The Shamanic Powers *of*
ROLLI...
THUNE...

"These first-person encounters with one of the most intriguing figures of recent American history are by turn frightening, amusing, informative, touching, and mystifying. Rolling Thunder's healing and wisdom were sought after by characters as diverse as members of the Grateful Dead, Muhammed Ali, and Buckminster Fuller. The authors have done us all a huge service by collecting these extraordinary accounts of a remarkable man."

CHRISTOPHER RYAN, PH.D., COAUTHOR OF THE
NEW YORK TIMES BESTSELLER *SEX AT DAWN*

"For any person who wants to expand their knowledge of rare and extraordinary powers and healing abilities exhibited by few on our planet and to learn of the remarkable Rolling Thunder's adept expression and application of such abilities—this book is a 'must-read.' Jaw-dropping awe and wonder will be a common response from many! And what a privilege to be reading compelling firsthand accounts by individuals who, each in their own right, contribute greatly to the education, upliftment, and enlightenment of many."

DEBBIE JOFFE ELLIS, M.D.A.M., PSYCHOLOGIST AND ADJUNCT PRO-
FESSOR OF PSYCHOLOGY AT COLUMBIA UNIVERSITY

"More than four decades have now passed since I first heard Rolling Thunder speak at a symposium in San Francisco sponsored by the Association for Humanistic Psychology. I have no doubt that Rolling Thunder's presence at this gathering of open-minded academics and therapists had been facilitated by Stanley Krippner.

So, it is both fascinating and heartening to see that, so many decades later, Krippner and his fellow consciousness explorers are still grappling with the spiritual mysteries, social implications, and theoretical dilemmas that have followed in the wake of Rolling Thunder's brilliant career as a Native American shaman. This book exhibits a depth of understanding beyond that of previous treatments. I highly recommend it."

JEFFREY MISHLOVE, PH.D.,
HOST OF NEW THINKING ALLOWED VIDEO CHANNEL

"The legendary Native American shaman Rolling Thunder captured the imagination of musicians, writers, and artists during his lifetime, and his legacy continues to inspire and captivate readers from all walks of life. . . . [a] fascinating retrospective look at a uniquely iconic medicine man. Simply put, you're in for a treat. Tune in, turn on, and read *The Shamanic Powers of Rolling Thunder.*"

STUART FISCHER, M.D., AUTHOR OF *THE PARK AVENUE DIET*

"Krippner and Jones have assembled a fascinating and inspiring tribute to Rolling Thunder. To be 'a living prayer' is what The White Buffalo Calf Woman of the Lakotas brought to all people. Rolling Thunder lived this truth, and the elements of nature responded in kind as so many people recount herein. His legacy reminds us all that each human's capacity and purpose, is to 'shamanize,' to be a co-creator."

J. ZOHARA MEYERHOFF HIERONIMUS, D.H.L.,
AUTHOR OF *THE FUTURE OF HUMAN EXPERIENCE*
AND COHOST OF *21ST CENTURY RADIO*

"An essential companion volume to *The Voice of Rolling Thunder* for anyone wanting to understand his life, the lives of those he touched, and the variety of disciplines he influenced."

MARK A. SCHROLL, PH.D., EDITOR OF *TRANSPERSONAL ECOSOPHY,*
VOL. 1: THEORY, METHODS, AND CLINICAL ASSESSMENTS

The Shamanic Powers *of*

ROLLING THUNDER

As Experienced by Alberto Villoldo, John Perry Barlow, Larry Dossey, and Others

Edited by Sidian Morning Star Jones and Stanley Krippner, Ph.D.

Bear & Company
Rochester, Vermont • Toronto, Canada

Bear & Company
One Park Street
Rochester, Vermont 05767
www.BearandCompanyBooks.com

Bear & Company is a division of Inner Traditions International

Library of Congress Cataloging-in-Publication Data
Names: Jones, Sidian Morning Star, editor.
Title: The Shamanic powers of Rolling Thunder : as experienced by Alberto
    Villoldo, John Perry Barlow, Larry Dossey, and others / edited by Sidian
    Morning Star Jones and Stanley Krippner, Ph.D.
Description: Rochester, Vermont : Bear & Company, 2016. | Includes
    bibliographical references.
Identifiers: LCCN 2016014037 (print) | LCCN 2016036031 (e-book) |
    ISBN 9781591432272 (pbk.) | ISBN 9781591432289 (e-book)
Subjects: LCSH: Rolling Thunder. | Shamanism—United States. | Indians of
    North America—Medicine. | Indians of North America—Religion. | Spiritual
    healing.
Classification: LCC BF1622.U6 S53 2016 (print) | LCC BF1622.U6 (e-book) |
    DDC 299.7—dc23
LC record available at https://lccn.loc.gov/2016014037

Printed and bound in the United States by Versa Press, Inc.

10 9 8 7 6 5 4 3 2 1

Text design by Debbie Glogover and layout by Priscilla Baker
This book was typeset in Garamond Premier Pro with Berling LT Std and Futura
Std for display fonts

To send correspondence to the authors of this book, mail a first-class letter to the author c/o Inner Traditions • Bear & Company, One Park Street, Rochester, VT 05767, and we will forward the communication, or contact Sidian Morning Star Jones directly at **sidianmorningstar@gmail.com** or **OpenSourceReligion.net** or Stanley Krippner directly through **www.stanleykrippner.weebly.com**.

Sidian Jones dedicates this book to Stanley Krippner, "the only person to fully accept me for who I am."

Stanley Krippner dedicates this book to Richard Adams, Thom Denomme, Betsy Easton, Harry Easton, Donna Eden, Howard Eisenberg, David Feinstein, Jay Friedheim, Kim Glenney, Scott Glenney, Bob Hieronimus, Zohara Hieronimus, Bob Hoss, Russell Jaffe, John Koo, Phil Pollack, Jimmy Smull, Gert Reutter, and Michael Winkler, "who know the reasons why."

Contents

PART 4

THUNDER ENCOUNTERS

PART 5

META TANTAY

Acknowledgments

The authors acknowledge the support of the Saybrook Chair for the Study of Consciousness for its financial support of this book's preparation. They would also like to thank Steve Hart and Rosemary Coffey for their editorial services and hard work, and Ron Boyer, Clint Evans, Katharine Fletcher, and Nina Zabelin for their work done on our previous Rolling Thunder book. The authors would also like to thank Jürgen Kremer for allowing us to use several of the drawings he executed during a visit to Meta Tantay.

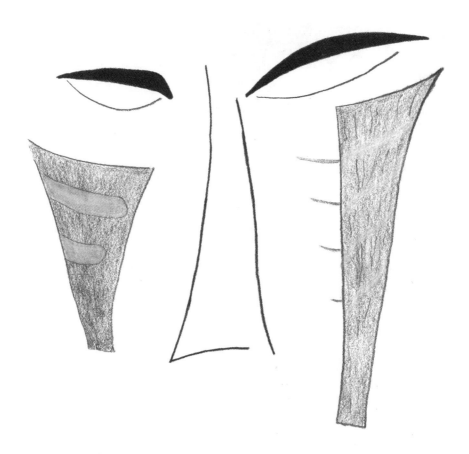

The more power you have, the more careful you have to be.

ROLLING THUNDER

Rolling Thunder as a Transpersonal and Transcultural Exemplar

Harris Friedman, Ph.D.

HARRIS FRIEDMAN, PH.D., is a practicing clinical and organizational consulting psychologist, as well as an active researcher. He recently retired as research professor of psychology at the University of Florida, where he remains on its courtesy faculty, and now teaches part-time at Goddard College, as well as supervises dissertations at several other universities. He has more than two hundred professional publications, many appearing in top scientific journals and garnering international media coverage. His most recent books include *Transcultural Competence* (2015), *The Praeger Handbook of Social Justice and Psychology, Vols. 1–3* (2014), and *The Wiley-Blackwell Handbook of Transpersonal Psychology* (2013). He is also senior editor of the *International Journal of Transpersonal Studies* and associate editor of *The Humanistic Psychologist*. As a Fellow of the American Psychological Association, he recently received the Abraham Maslow Award "given to an individual for an outstanding and lasting contribution to the exploration of the farther reaches of human spirit."

Rolling Thunder was a controversial Native American medicine man who passed away in 1997. He received considerable notoriety as a person who straddled both traditional Native American and modern Western culture, being willing to share his beliefs with all who came seeking healing and wisdom. This occurred during a time in which many cultural barriers were breaking down, as formerly insular beliefs began to be shared with the larger world. As an example, Bruce Lee, a charismatic Chinese kung fu practitioner, was initially criticized, and even physically accosted, by other Chinese kung fu masters for being one of the first from his tradition to teach this martial art outside of the Chinese community from which it arose (Gong 2014). Similarly, Rolling Thunder's willingness to share his teachings across cultural divides with the larger community of all people was noteworthy, and became a source of concern for some in Native American communities who did not want sacred knowledge transmitted to members of groups considered oppressive to Native Americans.

Although Rolling Thunder was a ceaseless advocate for Native American causes and was fully aware of the holocaust perpetrated upon Native people in America, he welcomed all with a warm embrace. In addition, he was able to focus his teachings and healings in ways that made them accessible to people who did not share his cultural background and, in this vein, exhibited a rare transcultural competence, an ability to recognize and respect cultural differences, as well as to reconcile them in ways that realized a beneficial and sustainable outcome for all (Glover and Friedman 2015). Insofar as his expressed stance toward reality was greatly expanded, as compared to the prevailing Western understandings, he also serves as an exemplar of a transpersonal approach (Friedman and Hartelius 2013), referring to his world view in which the profound interconnectedness of all reality was held paramount.

Sidian Jones and Stanley Krippner's second volume on Rolling

Thunder consists mainly of stories about this medicine man, and follows their earlier volume (Jones and Krippner 2012) by richly providing many examples of his proclivity for amazing people. One after another, these extraordinary individuals testify to unusual encounters with this extraordinary person. A few even describe the influence he had on their lives through nonphysical encounters, such as in dreams, and some who had never met him claimed to have sensed his presence in unusual ways. The majority of stories, however, focus on direct interactions in which Rolling Thunder often seemed to transcend conventional understanding.

The most ubiquitous of these stories relate to Rolling Thunder's assumed name. Although named John Pope at birth, he became known as Rolling Thunder for a reason, namely his apparent interconnectedness with the weather, especially his reputed ability to summon forth intense rainstorms accompanied by thunder. He could do this even in unlikely circumstances when such occurrences defied current meteorological conditions. In this book, numerous accounts focus on Rolling Thunder's accurate prediction of such weather events in ways implying that he had successfully manipulated them for some purpose.

In a previous book with Krippner (Krippner and Friedman 2010), we distinguished between extraordinary events and experiences, limiting our discussion to understanding psychic and other nonordinary experiences, including examining their neurobiological concomitants, while bracketing the ontological reality of any reported events associated with these experiences. In the case of supposedly bringing forth thunder in a consistent way during numerous unlikely occasions with multiple people experiencing this phenomenon, the evidence appears credible that something extraordinary happened with considerable consistency in relationship to this aptly named medicine man and the weather. The many reported events of thunderstorms that literally arose from blue skies in otherwise dry conditions are unlikely to have been confabulated events, given that the presence of thunder is clearer than that of a bell. Thus is it improbable that the phenomena were widely misperceived.

Sleight of hand and hypnosis also seem unreasonable explanations for these doings. The rub involves whether Rolling Thunder was able to predict these thunderous events in ways that cannot be understood through normal means and, more interestingly, whether he was in some way responsible for them.

There are many naturalistic ways to predict the weather that can seem uncanny to an untutored observer. For example, it is often claimed that once one becomes "attuned to the sky, the air, and animal behaviors, it's possible to predict the weather quite reliably" (Wikihow 2015). In addition, many people experience unusual physical signs related to weather changes, such as arthritic pain related to falling barometric pressure and lowering temperature (Arthritis Foundation 2015). All of these naturalistic explanations could account for Rolling Thunder's noted ability to proclaim the advent of thunderstorms, and he may have used these skills to appear to have magical powers.

Although it may be impossible to ever ascertain whether or not Rolling Thunder could predict, as well as control, weather events in nonordinary ways, it is clear that he impressed many people with the skills related to his assumed name. The numerous stories about his use of these, and many other, unusual talents contained within Sidian Jones and Stanley Krippner's book adds to the mystique of Rolling Thunder. Regardless of whether he had predictive power or control over thunder and other events, Rolling Thunder undeniably influenced the experiences and belief systems of many who encountered him in person and through what some described in other interactions. This book adds to the important anecdotal literature on anomalous experience (Cardeña, Lynn, and Krippner 2013), as well as makes inspiring reading about the life of a truly remarkable transcultural and transpersonal exemplar.

INTRODUCTION
Magic, Myth, and Rolling Thunder

Stanley Krippner, Ph.D.

STANLEY KRIPPNER, PH.D., is the Alan Watts Professor of Psychology at Saybrook University in Oakland, California, and past president of the Association for Humanistic Psychology and the International Association for the Study of Dreams. The recipient of several distinguished awards and the author and coauthor of many books, including *The Voice of Rolling Thunder* with Sidian Morning Star Jones, *Demystifying Shamans and Their World* with Adam Rock, *Personal Mythology*, and *Extraordinary Dreams and How to Work with Them*, he lives in San Rafael, California.

Over the years, I paid several visits to Meta Tantay, the 262-acre spiritual community organized by Rolling Thunder and his wife Spotted Fawn in a Nevada desert. It flourished from 1978 to 1985, attracting such visitors as Joan Baez, Joni Mitchell, Buckminster Fuller, Candice Bergen, and Muhammad Ali. Rolling Thunder and his friends had bought the land with the help of Mickey Hart and his band, the Grateful Dead, the popular rock group. Mickey's friendship with Rolling Thunder had paved the way for my first encounter with him several years earlier.

One evening, RT, as he was called in Meta Tantay, took me to the very edge of the property and began to howl. This was not a brief yelp, but a long sustained howl that seemed to start from his belly and empty his lungs as it resonated into the chilly night air. Had I not known of RT's "medicine ways," I would have thought he had gone over the edge.

Taking this behavior in stride, I soon heard a similar howl. A few minutes later, several coyotes appeared and walked so close to us that I could have petted them had I been so disposed. As the leader of the pack approached RT, the two of them howled back and forth at each other. After this interaction, the coyotes disappeared into the mist. RT remarked, "Every so often, I renew the bargain. The coyotes will not raid our chicken coops if we ensure their safety when we see them on our land. So far, they have kept their end of the bargain and so have we."

In 1982 I heard that a coyote had been hit by a passing automobile but was rescued by residents of Meta Tantay. Named Ejipah by the community, the coyote was treated for a concussion by RT. After two months Ejipah had become quite tame and never bit or snapped at any community member. Eventually Ejipah was released into the wild, following a ritual conducted by RT designed to enable her to be reaccepted into the coyote band. RT commented that since coyotes have families and tribes of their own, there was no reason why they could not be good neighbors of the Meta Tantay family. For several months, during which Ejipah could be seen just north of Meta Tantay, she was assumed to be part of the band that "sang" near the community every night, a ritual that became a part of the Meta Tantay tradition.

RITUALS AND MYTHS

I realized that I had also witnessed an interspecies ritual that, like all rituals, had a purpose. RT explained that coyotes keep the rat and mouse population down. They also feed on rabbits, preventing them from destroying Meta Tantay's vegetable gardens. Elsewhere in Nevada where farmers have killed much of the coyote population, their chickens and gardens have suffered as a result. *Meta Tantay*, a Chumash term meaning "go in peace," typifies my observations of RT and the coyotes.

Aboriginal tribes in Australia speak of the dreamtime, a mythical era when humans and animals lived peacefully with each other and even spoke in a mutually comprehensible way. Other Native cultures venerate this sort of connection as well, not only with animals but also with birds, fish, amphibians, and reptiles. A shaman's "power animal" can be called upon for assistance, and animal spirits often appear in the dreams of medicine people. Medicine men and women may wear animal skins, bones, teeth, and claws during their rituals.

A ritual is actually a mythic performance. Rituals are meant to influence either the external world—as when RT performed a rain dance in an attempt to end a drought—or the internal world, as when RT led his community in a "snake dance" to mobilize energy for a healing session. Both dances were infused with magical action, a type of activity that has its own set of rules in addition to those recognized by Western cause-and-effect concepts. William Irwin Thompson, a cultural historian, has written about how performance can either open new horizons for the future or close them down.

This concept resembles what David Feinstein and I have described as the difference between an old myth, which is no longer functional, and a new myth, which is eager to supplant it. For example, the European invasion of the Americas brought with it the new myth of Christianity, one that supplanted hundreds of indigenous old myths. In a few places there was a synthesis, as when African slaves cleverly combined their mythology with Roman Catholicism in what today are Brazil, Puerto Rico, Cuba, Haiti, and the Dominican Republic. But this synthesis never occurred on a large scale in the United States and Canada, leading to a mythic turmoil whose devastating effects, such as alcoholism and spousal abuse, can be seen to this day.

MAGIC

Western technology emerged from magic, but left out anything that could not be easily explained by its own rules and regulations. The physicist Luc Sala has observed that this is what differentiates ritual from ceremony—that is, rituals remain linked to magic, whereas ceremonies have social and psychological functions. Coronation ceremonies, graduation ceremonies, and wedding ceremonies can be colorful, impressive, and even grandiose—but they lack the depth and mystery that adhere to even the simplest of rituals.

Some people would dispute this differentiation. For example, RT often invited me to one of his sunrise ceremonies, using the word *ceremony* instead of *ritual*. He would surely dispute the allegation that his hailing of the morning sun was devoid of deep significance and mystery. After Bob Dylan attended one of RT's sunrise ceremonies, he was so impressed that he invited RT to some of his concerts.

Luc Sala also has provided a useful definition of *magic:* He differentiated the sacred dimension of reality from the ordinary dimension. Magic links the two dimensions, putting this link to practical use through intention, the same intention that can be found in rituals. Indeed, each magical act involves a ritual of some sort. Rolling Thunder is reputed to have been able to block his image from a photograph that was taken without his permission. If this was the case, it would have been a magical act, something done with intention and a simple ritual involving mentally removing his image from the film.

The anthropologist Charles Laughlin has used the term *ritualization* to refer to the tendency of humans and other animals to initiate a sequence of behaviors to communicate information or to complete a task. Examples are threat displays among gorillas, mating displays among birds, and coyote "sings," such as the one I witnessed at Meta Tantay. For Laughlin, a *ritual* is more complex than ritualization and is more likely to be carried out with some degree of intention, or conscious awareness. *Ceremonies*, to Laughlin, are formalized, complex rituals conducted with a great deal of awareness such as a Catholic Mass or a Jewish sitting shiva. They invariably involve *symbols,* images that take on a deeper and often unconscious meaning. For example, the coyote regularly takes on the role of a trickster in some Native American traditions, while the bear is frequently seen as a healer.

Perhaps this is why RT spoke of sunrise ceremonies. Clearly, the rising sun was more than an astronomical event. It symbolized the beginning of a new day, a new project, or a new way of being in the world. The anthropologist Michael Harner has observed that the power animals that appear in dreams and visions often use symbols to deliver messages to shamans and medicine people. But the symbol is specific to the culture; thus, an image of the Madonna would have a different meaning to a Latin American *curandera* from what it would to an Amazonian *paje* who had never heard of Mary and Jesus.

In my experience, Rolling Thunder never spoke about miracles, those reported events that transcend the laws of nature. To RT, even the most incredible healings followed natural laws, although Western science had yet to discover them. The Native American poet Sherman Alexie, in a *TIME* magazine interview, remarked, "I don't believe in magic, but I do believe in interpreting coincidence exactly the way you want. I woke up after a tremendous bender, and the acceptance for my first book of poems was in the mailbox. For me, it was a call to get sober" (Luscombe 2012, 76). Noah Nez, in his column Native Skeptic added that "there are rituals and ceremonies dedicated to 'welcoming' and 'celebrating' the rain, [but] this does not imply that the dances themselves bring, or cause, the rain" (Nez 2013, 9–11). Rolling Thunder often told me that while he interacted with nature, he did not attempt to control or change nature.

MYTHS AND MAGIC

Myths almost always contain a magical component, whether they deal with bewitched princesses, seductive sirens, or adventurous wizards.

The mythologist Joseph Campbell pointed out that myths have many functions, one of which is an attempt to explain the workings of nature. When science claimed to do it better, the Western world equated myth with superstition. There were still anomalies that mainstream science could not explain, but when parapsychologists offered assistance, they were branded pseudoscientists and ignored (at best) or derided (at worst).

Just as magic led to technology, myth led to science—the disciplined inquiry that tries to explore and explain the nature of the inner and outer worlds. Myths were created by primordial humans not only to construct a cosmology but also to help prehistoric people find their niche in the social order, establish a society's rules of conduct, and assist transitions between childhood and maturity, between sickness and health, and between life and death. These latter functions grew out of the mythological creation stories and the cosmology that described a lawful, well-organized universe.

In ancient times, magic and myth engaged in a perennial dance, one that was expressed in rituals, which provided protection against human and nonhuman enemies, above and beyond the use of weapons. Magic and myth were expressed in healing sessions, including but not limited to herbal brews, poultices, salves, and ointments, many of which had ingredients that make sense even to today's pharmacologists and physicians. Those remedies that were biochemically inert often worked because of the so-called placebo effect, indicating that suggestibility was an adaptive trait. People who did not respond to shamanic ministrations died, their genes dropped out of the gene pool, and the survivors passed on their suggestion-prone capacities to their descendants.

Rolling Thunder told the anthropologist Jim Swan about a dream that demonstrates his immersion in mythology. As a young man, he dreamed that he was standing before a shining golden portal. The door swung open, revealing Quetzalcoatl, the mythic hero of present-day Mexico. Quetzalcoatl, who was known for his benevolent reign, is the central figure in many stories, in some of which he shape-shifts into a feathered serpent. In this dream, Quetzalcoatl merged into RT's body amidst a brilliant golden light. RT told Swan that he had awakened in tears, feeling that his entire body was on fire. For the next three days, whenever RT touched someone, that person would experience an electric shock. He interpreted this dream as a call to become a medicine man. Indeed, it is typical of many "initiation dreams" that have been reported by shamans and medicine people.

MYTHS AND SCIENCE

Measurement and language were the devices that transformed myth into science and magic into technology. If a mythological explanation of a natural phenomenon was accurate, that accuracy could be measured. If a magical incantation produced the desired results, those results could be measured. The mythological description of celestial bodies was replaced by the calendars of Babylonian scholars and by the even more accurate calendars of Mayan astronomers. The magical rituals conducted to ensure germination of seeds were tested by observing which seeds sprouted most profusely under which procedures. Measurements needed to be precise to determine the correct proportion of the components of ayahuasca and other psychedelic brews that took their drinkers to other worlds. Finally, the mythic construction of those worlds provided the inebriants road maps that would help them navigate the Upper World, the Lower World, and all the parallel universes to which they were transported.

Measurement depends on language for its expression and its application. Measurement and language coalesce in numerals, which permit quantification and calculation. When a Native American shaman placed beads on a string to record the number of days since something had been planted, this was an example of quantifying time. When a shaman in central Mexico determined the number of years needed to deconstruct and rebuild a pyramid, this required calculation. This information was conveyed to tribal architects so that they could initiate the process. Numerals also were used to predict the year in which Quetzalcoatl would return from his voyage across the sea; this was a cyclical, not a linear, prediction, and every several years scouts gathered on the shore of the Caribbean, watching for unusual signs. The Spanish conquistador Hernán Cortés arrived at exactly the predicted time, assuring him a hero's welcome instead of armed resistance.

Information is the outcome of measurement and is expressed in language. Hence, there is an ongoing dance between measurement and language, just as there is a dance between magic and myth. William Irwin Thompson has written eloquently about the role of language in human evolution, claiming that storytelling is an inescapable feature of human existence. If it is measurement that helps turn myth into science, it is storytelling that returns the compliment. Without this return, humanity becomes separated from nature, and knowledge diverges from myth. This separation results in a distortion of history. "The very language we use to discuss the past speaks of tools, hunters, and *men,* when every statue and painting we discover cries out to us that [early] humanity was a culture of art, the love of animals, and women" (Thompson 1981, 102).

Language determines how a culture and its inhabitants construct their world. There were hundreds of Native American languages prior to the European invasion, and they were characterized by incredible diversity. However, most of them used verbs in ways that English-speaking people would use nouns; campfire stories were often told from the perspective of an animal, and when tribal leaders met, they used many gestures and hand movements to convey meaning when they did not share a spoken language. Native American languages can be described as "embodied," as infused with metaphor, and as close to nature.

In general, women were given a voice in tribal councils; RT often reminded his audiences that the Clan Mother could be more powerful than a chief. Social scientists Sharon Mijares, Alina Rafea, Rachael Falik, and Jenny Eda Schipper have documented the destructive results of patriarchy, which they claim supplanted egalitarian societies in most of the world around 4000 BCE. Organized religion took the place of shamanism and local spiritual rituals. Females were considered less important than males, and animals were seen as a commodity to be exploited, along with the rest of nature, rather than something to be nurtured. Transformational art, such as the cave murals that still exist in southwest Europe and southern Africa, was probably evoked by local psychedelics in rituals celebrating the bond among humans, their fellow animals, and the Earth that they all inhabited.

Claude Lévi-Strauss, one of the leading scholars of mythology in the twentieth century, saw myth as a "popular science" that enabled people to understand what was going on in the natural and social world. This understanding could come about through scientific inquiry or through the imagination. Even so, Lévi-Strauss contended that the latter approach could be just as rigorous as the former, and that the two could work together, especially when scientific inquiry fell short of providing an explanation of crucial issues such as resolving contradictions and dichotomies like life and death as well as the bonds between humans and nature.

MAGIC AND TECHNOLOGY

Restoring these bonds was Rolling Thunder's mission. The extent of his success is the theme of this book. Rolling Thunder was not averse to technology; for example, Meta Tantay utilized solar power to generate energy. Nor did he shy away from scientific inquiry; he was willing to put himself on the line when a formal investigation was offered. In 1975, Jean Millay was invited to demonstrate a biofeedback light structure at the Congress of Witchcraft in Bogotá, Colombia, which was exploring the connection between magic and technology. Coincidentally, the Association for Humanistic Psychology (AHP) was holding its annual conference in Colorado at the same time. Jean invited Rolling Thunder to arrange a special sunrise ceremony that would provide an additional intercontinental link. She also invited Seucucui, an Abiuticuan Mamu from Colombia, to join her group, and James Dowlen, an artist residing in California, to provide a fourth link. Seucucui was asked to lead a meditation that would link the groups together.

I was a member of the AHP group, whose instructions were to build a fire on a nearby hill and throw "oracle coins" to obtain a six-line hexagram from the I Ching—an ancient Chinese collection of short verses. The verse known as the Wanderer, which matched the coins, contains two major images: fire and mountain (one for the top trigram, one for the bottom trigram). Not knowing that these particular images were in the verse selected, both images were cited by either Jean or a member of her group—as were other images as well. Rolling Thunder reported the image of an eagle from his group, and Dowlen drew two pages of images, some of which resembled the hexagram and some of which did not.

Perhaps the most unusual aspect of this transcontinental attempt to capture magic was displayed by the weather. As Jean and her group drove from Bogotá to Lake Guatavita, the predetermined site of the adventure, there was an unexpected and incessant rain. However, it stopped just as the group reached the lake. Jean was the only member of her group who knew that Rolling Thunder had a legendary reputation for interacting with the weather. At the end of the session, Seucucui invited Jean to his village, where she reported that "everything seemed to hold the essence of magic." Hence, Jean, who had brought modern technology to Colombia, ended up becoming immersed in magic, or at least a reasonable facsimile thereof. Moreover, she returned with a fascinating story, one that involved the ubiquitous Rolling Thunder.

Rolling Thunder used storytelling to instruct and to entertain, to heal the sick and to arouse to action. His presentations included drumming, singing, and occasionally a Native American mentalist. In addition, Rolling Thunder never hesitated to remind his audiences of Native American prophecies, many of them dire predictions of the catastrophes that would befall humanity if the destruction of Earth continued.

The impact of Rolling Thunder did not stop with his death. His message lives on, and the exploitation of nature, once taken for granted as a human prerogative, is being challenged more frequently and more directly than ever before in modern times. Magic became technology and myth became science. However, technology without a touch of magic becomes mechanistic, and science without a mythic subtext becomes reductionistic. Mechanism and reductionism have brought Earth and its inhabitants to a critical point in history. The survival of Earth's rain forests is at risk; the planet's air and oceans are increasingly polluted. The Cree Indians call this universal madness *wetiko,* a loss of spirit. What is needed is a critical mass to reverse the trend before the most apocalyptic of Native American prophecies comes to pass.

THE RUNNING COYOTE

In 1989, Mickey Hart (who had introduced me to RT in 1970) reached me by phone, saying that we needed to fly to Nevada because RT's daughter was concerned about her father's health. Shocked by his appearance, Mickey and I persuaded him to board the private plane we had secured, flying him to San Francisco, where Mickey's own physician took charge of a series of operations that saved RT's life.

A few weeks later, I received a lovely letter from Carrie Spotted Eagle, one of RT's housemates. She wrote, "Thank you, Stanley, for a job well done. Your obvious love and concern were a pleasure to behold as well as the gentleness with which your words were spoken. I appreciate more than anything your calmness and respect during what could have been a chaotic mess. Our days here are filled with peace, quietness, and lots of love. The only thing missing is RT and it will be wonderful having him home again."

She continued, "I was out for a walk with my two-month-old wolf-cross puppy, Miyaca, and decided that life is great here in Carlin. We saw a beautiful coyote running in the bush along the riverbank, and egrets and a small whirlwind that touched the river sending water swirling and flying all over the place. Summer has arrived and the garden is ready for planting tomorrow. It is good. Ho!"

Rather than being terrified by the coyote, Carrie Spotted Eagle enjoyed its presence, since it was part of the natural landscape. Was it RT's "bargain" that enabled the coyote to run free along the river-bank? I recalled once more that some Native American traditions see the coyote as a trickster, one who plays tricks on humans to remind them that they live in a world of complexity and ambiguity. Sidian and I hope that the readers of this book will savor its stories, many of which are complex and ambiguous. Our readers also need to use their critical judgment and common sense in evaluating what they read. We are well aware that there are many scholars, some of them Native Americans, who consider RT to be a trickster himself. But the stories in this book were not told by RT but by those who were impacted by him.

RT never claimed to be perfect. However, the role he played in the lives of our storytellers demonstrates that positive change and transformation can come from a variety of sources, some of which are checkered and imperfect, but—nonetheless—potent, practical, and life affirming.

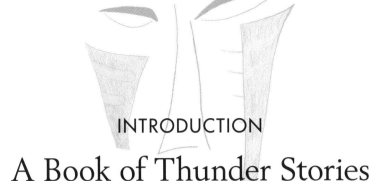

INTRODUCTION

A Book of Thunder Stories

Sidian Morning Star Jones

SIDIAN MORNING STAR JONES, Rolling Thunder's grandson and one of the caretakers of his spiritual legacy, is a graphic designer, inventor, and founder of My Mythos (mymythos.org), a website that allows people to compare their personal myths. He is also the founder of Open Source Religion (www.opensourcereligion.com), a platform to help people define and refine their beliefs. Coauthor of *The Voice of Rolling Thunder* with Stanley Krippner, he lives in Boise, Idaho.

I met my grandfather only a few times, but each encounter left a strong impression on me. He was an imposing figure who evoked awe and respect. On one occasion, he gave me a tomahawk to hold. This simple act had meaning for me because it felt very symbolic of passing down his tradition to the next generation.

It was not until Stanley and I were writing our 2012 book, *The Voice of Rolling Thunder,* that I discovered facts about my grandfather that I had never known. One of our interviewees told us that my great-grandfather (Rolling Thunder's father) belonged to a Cherokee group of activists called Snake and was killed during one of their protests. His father's name was Yank Killer, and my great-grandfather took the same name.

THE STORY OF ROLLING THUNDER

Rolling Thunder was born John Pope on September 19, 1916, and his mother was Caucasian. He grew up on a reservation in Oklahoma and began to learn the ways of medicine people at an early age, having been called to the Red Road of Service in many of his dreams. He led a laborer's life, working as a brakeman for the Southern Pacific Railroad. He married a Mohawk woman named Marlene. They had three children and settled in a trailer home in Carlin, Nevada.

One day the trailer caught on fire and Marlene ran back to save their baby. My grandfather ran after her but to no avail—both she and the baby died. My grandfather suffered severe burns and the physicians told him that both his hands would have to be amputated. But he had a vision about a medicine plant that could be found in the Nevada mountains. He found the plant and claimed that it started to glow when he approached it. He made a poultice of this plant that saved both his hands, but the scars remained for the rest of his life.

My studies of shamanism and Native healers have shown me that this is a recurring pattern. Many healers are called by their dreams, and others are called by curing themselves of a serious illness. Both of these callings were experienced by my grandfather. Once called, a medicine man or medicine woman has to study, and my grandfather learned Indian Medicine from Silver Wolf and Phillip Grey Horse, both of whom lived in Nevada. Later, he learned additional skills from Frank Fools Crow, Mad Bear Anderson, Aminitrus Seputoia, and David Monongye.

In the meantime, he married Spotted Fawn, a Western Shoshone Indian, and he was adopted into that tribe. They had six children, four of whom survived. One of them was my mother. Neither Rolling

Thunder nor his children registered as Native Americans with the federal Bureau of Indian Affairs. My grandfather took this action in the spirit of his father's protest band, the Chickamauga Cherokee, who had refused to register with the bureau. This refusal led many anthropologists and even Native American officials to doubt my grandfather's Native authenticity, but Rolling Thunder was stubborn, and once he made a decision he stuck to it.

Stanley had been introduced to my grandfather by Mickey Hart, a percussionist for the Grateful Dead rock group. In 1971, Stanley invited Rolling Thunder to speak at a conference sponsored by the Menninger Foundation in Topeka, Kansas. It was there that Rolling Thunder met American journalist and author Doug Boyd and invited Boyd to Carlin for a visit. Boyd's subsequent book about the experience created international attention (Boyd 1974), allowing Rolling Thunder to retire from his job on the railroad and devote himself to the Red Road of Service. He traveled around the United States, Canada, and Western Europe, telling people about Native American traditions and teachings. With the assistance of Spotted Fawn, he founded Meta Tantay, a spiritual community that flourished for a decade.

When Spotted Fawn passed, Rolling Thunder went into deep mourning. Meta Tantay fell apart and my grandfather's health deteriorated. He married his nurse, who took the name of Carmen Sun Rising Pope, and who produced a book of transcripts of my grandfather's lectures after he passed in 1997 (Pope 1999).

THUNDER WEATHER, THUNDER HEALING, THUNDER PEOPLE, AND THUNDER ENCOUNTERS

My grandfather often talked about the Thunder People, those who shared his vision of a natural way of life. He even prescribed a Thunder Diet of healthy foods combined with clean living and keen thinking. It is in this spirit that we have clustered the stories in this book into four groups: Thunder Weather, Thunder Healing, Thunder People, and Thunder Encounters. Several of the book's contributors share more than one story in these pages.

The Thunder Weather chapters describe my grandfather's interaction with the forces of nature, in particular thunder and lightning. Alberto Villoldo and Larry Dossey met my grandfather and relate experiences that some dismiss as remarkable coincidences. We will let our readers decide for themselves. Phillip Scott, Bill Storm, and Karel Bouse never met RT but still felt his presence during unusual and sudden shifts in the weather.

The Thunder Healing chapters describe RT's different "doctoring" episodes, some of them too remarkable to be explained by placebo and expectation effects. Stephan Schwartz's description of the "mist wolf" that appeared during RT's doctoring of a young boy was witnessed by several people, one of whom confirmed Stephan's account in our previous book (Jones and Krippner 2012). Karie Garnier is convinced that his life was saved by RT's doctoring. Unlike the one-session "mist wolf" healing, this one took several months to complete. Jean Millay and John Perry Barlow describe two very different types of so-called exorcisms, one in California and one in Wyoming, while Brian Wilkes vividly portrays a healing that occurred in tandem with a recurring dream.

The Thunder People chapters depict my grandfather's interaction with men and women who had significant interactions with him. He helped these individuals walk the Red Road of Service to humankind and Earth. Ed Little Crow, Kenneth Cohen, Carolyna Saint Germain, and Kanya Vashon McGhee have changed many people's lives for the better. Their ranks could also include Carolyna's husband, Norman Cohen, who adds a few anecdotes to her chapter, as well as the Native or partially Native authors of several other chapters such as Leslie Gray, Oh Shinna Fast Wolf, and Phillip Scott, and people of other ethnicities. Richard Nixon makes a cameo appearance in these chapters. RT reminded his audiences that people, including himself, are a mixture of positives and negatives, and Nixon had at least one redeeming virtue, namely his work on behalf of Native Americans.

Rolling Thunder speaks for himself in the interview conducted by Jean Millay.

The Thunder Encounter stories take a variety of forms. Some of them focus on a particular incident, such as those written by William Lyon, Jean Millay, Tom Eelkema, Walter Peterson, and Michael Austin. Other encounters, such as those noted by Michael Neils, Jürgen Kremer, Gert Reutter, and David Sessions, cover a longer span of time. Leslie Gray and Oh Shinna Fast Wolf knew my grandfather quite well and provide illuminating overviews. Several of these encounters are included in the Meta Tantay stories, which highlight the importance of my grandmother's impact on this community.

Stories are almost as essential to people's lives as food, clothing, and shelter. Stories provide meaning. Stories provide direction. And stories provide entertainment. Stanley and I hope that the stories in this book will provide all three. My grandfather loved to tell Thunder Stories and he would have enjoyed knowing that people still remember him and continue to tell stories about the impact he made on their lives.

PART 1

Thunder Weather

Spiritual force is much greater than the force of physical violence.

ROLLING THUNDER

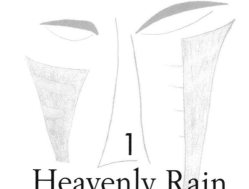

1
Heavenly Rain
with Rolling Thunder

Alberto Villoldo, Ph.D.

ALBERTO VILLOLDO, PH.D., is a medical anthropologist who has studied the healing practices of Amazonian and Andean shamans. Villoldo directs the Four Winds Society, where he trains individuals in the United States and Europe in the practice of shamanic energy medicine. He is the founder of the Light Body School, which has campuses in New York, California, and Germany, where he trains practitioners in energy medicine. He is the author of several books, including *Shaman, Healer, Sage; The Four Insights; Courageous Dreaming;* and *Power Up Your Brain.* We wrote him at his home in Chile, asking how RT had impacted his life. This is his reply.

We had been in ceremony with Rolling Thunder for three days. It had not rained for weeks. This is how it is in the desert in northern Nevada. A few sporadic rains in the wet season, and then parching heat for months.

That night we drove to the desert, far from the city lights and the power lines, to a sandy flat surrounded by clipped dunes, the place for our fire ceremony. Already about forty of us, whites and Indians, had gathered to pray and gaze quietly at the stars in the cloudless night. A bit later, RT, as we called him when he was not watching, pulled up in a beat-up pickup truck. The Shoshone medicine man stepped out of the cab, adjusted the straw hat that never seemed to leave his head, and strode to the circle.

As one of his helpers lit the fire RT explained that we were going to do a serpent dance, circling the flames slowly, releasing with each round the lifelessness inside each one of us—the way the serpent sheds her skin.

"All at once," he said. "Not like white people like to do, one scale at a time, so they can feel something." I could imagine him grinning under the starlight, chewing on his pipe.

"Shed the old skin," he said.

I thought we had already done this two days earlier, when he led us in an all-night sweat lodge. I had a bad sunburn, and was literally peeling off my skin as we spent hours sweating and singing. But he meant the other skin, the one we wear over our hearts, the carefully crafted persona, the face we "keep in a jar by the door," as the Beatles said.

DANCING OUR OLD SKINS AWAY

We danced into the night that night, circling the fire, with each revolution shedding a little of the past that festered within us like an old sore that would not heal. With each song we became less "civilized," less invested in the ways of the city, less suburban, and reclaimed our aboriginal soul. We slowly discovered we are all children of this Earth as we danced the way our ancestors had done for millennia. *We are all aboriginal,* I silently repeated to myself as I danced.

The serpent has gotten a bad rap in the West. We associate it with evil, with our being cast out of Eden. But for the medicine man the serpent is the primeval life force, representing sensuality and earthiness.

As with so many ancient cultures, RT considered the serpent sacred. Its power and medicine allowed us to heal ourselves and others. Perhaps this is why even in the West we have it as the symbol of healing in the caduceus of medicine.

When we were done I felt lighter than I had in years.

"It's customary after a dance to have a brief shower to erase our footprints," the old Indian explained. "Just so the white man does not think a bunch of savages have been out dancing and drinkin' and howling at the stars . . . "

And then the seemingly impossible happened. A light drizzle began, but there was not a single cloud in the sky. And then a full-blown rainstorm ensued, so that all of us got drenched as we ran to our vehicles. When we returned to camp I looked at Stanley Krippner, my professor at the time, and wondered if I had dreamt the whole scene with the rain. Yet he was as soaked as I was. That's when I realized that the weather had responded to Rolling Thunder, and I understood how he got his name.

A DREAM BIGGER THAN HIMSELF

RT would speak about the white man the way a father speaks about a wayward child. He had no bitterness, although the European settlers had taken his people's land and relocated his ancestors to disease-ridden reservations. He could see the folly of the ways of the Europeans, how greed and lust for power drove them to spoil Earth, on which they live. No other creature fouls its own nest the way we do.

Someday we will all have to explain our actions to the Great Spirit, settle our accounts with life, and our brief stint on Earth will be weighed on the scale of divine justice. Or so I remember RT saying. He explained that this is why it is important that we use our medicine, our gifts, for good, and that we touch everyone with a blessing; that we bring beauty to the world every chance we get.

"It's a long way down the ladder," he would explain.

His message did not remain confined to the reservation. Many of us were touched by the audacity of a brakeman for the railroad who was a master healer and medicine man, a poor Indian who dared to have a dream bigger than himself, or than his own people or his era. Even in the nightmare of that moment in history, with the growing oppression of indigenous people around the globe, he held fast to the dream of a world-that-could-be.

RT would occasionally visit Mickey Hart's ranch in Novato, California. Mickey, one of the drummers for the Grateful Dead, would later produce an album titled *Rolling Thunder,* in which the medicine man's distinct voice appears on the first track. In the wild and uninhibited music of the time, the album carried the medicine man's haunting message to millions of people. He was equally at ease with popular musicians and Hollywood celebrities of the time as he was with the poor who came to his humble home in Carlin, Nevada, for hope and healing.

His message that Spirit responds to your intentions, that nature supports your acts of courage and answers your prayers, was brought to the world by the Grateful Dead and by books such as the *Realms of Healing* that Krippner and I later coauthored (1976). And it was offered freely, gently, to everyone who met him. It was not only the thunder and wind that responded when he called—he also had a way of summoning the storms within you and leading you to the calm eye at the very center, which cleansed your wounds and healed your heart.

He did that for me.

Back then, I was a young man full of hope and fire. I recognized RT as an old man who had little trust in the ways of the white man yet continued to work tirelessly to bring peace and healing to everyone he met, Indian and white.

My days with the old Indian launched me on a twenty-five-year journey to explore the teachings of shamans of the Andes and the Amazon. Even in the most remote villages I visited in the Andes I would meet medicine men and women as dedicated to dreaming a healed world into being as Rolling Thunder was.

I am an old man now, and see little hope for humanity if Earth is to survive the avarice and shortsightedness of our people. Climate change, war, plague, and disease give me little cause for hope. And eventually one loses the optimism of youth. Yet I try to walk in RT's footsteps, to bring a little healing to those around me every day. I try to see beauty where others see only ugliness. I also try to inspire the young men and women I teach to dare to dream a bigger dream and create a better world, one where we live in harmony and peace with each other and with the land—a world in which we can hear the voice of Spirit all around us.

And with a smile I recall the memories of the times with RT and Stanley in the desert, that night when the sky opened up and the rain fell out of nowhere, and left us drenched in holy water for the rest of our lives.

2
How Rolling Thunder Made the Thunder Roll

Larry Dossey, M.D.

LARRY DOSSEY, M.D., is the author of a dozen books about the role of consciousness and spirituality in health, including *One Mind*, *Healing Words*, and *The Extraordinary Healing Power of Ordinary Things*. He is the executive editor of *Explore: The Journal of Science and Healing*. He sent us an account of what he learned from his encounter with RT.

THE PRACTICAL SHAMAN

During the early 1980s, and at the height of his popularity, Rolling Thunder was invited to give a talk at Unity of Dallas Church, which was just down the street from my office in the Medical City Dallas Hospital. A friend of mine called me on Friday morning of the day of RT's lecture and told me that RT wanted to see a doctor. Would I see him? Of course. So he and a retinue of three or four Native Americans in big hats and Western dress were escorted by my nurse down the hall to my office area around 4:00 p.m. that afternoon.

The nurse was carrying a chart (you can't see the doctor without a chart!) that was labeled THUNDER, ROLLING. I felt I knew Rolling Thunder somewhat through Doug Boyd's book, so I escorted him into my private office, not an exam room, out of respect and admiration, where we had a chat about his visit. And then he told me he had severe neck pain from craning his head into microphones at an unnatural angle (due to lots of recent speaking engagements) and desired some help for it.

He was very vague, however, and I had no idea what sort of help he expected. What does an internist do for a famous shaman? It was getting late in the day and patients were stacking up and I had to move things along. So we went into an exam room. A brief exam yielded normal results so I was still confused. Why would a famous shaman need to see an internist? Finally, seriously needing to move on, I followed a hunch and simply asked him how he felt about using pharmaceutical drugs. He smiled and implied that was why he had come.

So I went into our drug storage area and got three prescription drugs—a muscle relaxant, an anti-inflammatory medication, and some pain medication; all free samples left by drug company representatives—to help him get through his talk that night. As I gave him this little stash, he was clearly delighted and grateful. I felt I had met his expectations and that he had left in a happy frame of mind. This experience was an excellent demonstration of shamanic practicality on his part: don't get stuck in ideology; use what works.

But it wasn't over. As I escorted RT from my office, we bumped into a general surgeon who was a good friend of mine. The surgeon stopped in the narrow hallway and said hello. While I introduced them, RT looked the surgeon up and down with a keen eye. Then RT said, out of the blue and without any introductory comment, "Do you eat a lot of greens?" This particular surgeon was the only surgeon I knew who was a strict vegetarian. He was speechless. RT and I continued down the hallway, leaving the vegetarian surgeon openmouthed. RT had touched another human being, who would never forget the encounter. And it was great theater besides.

A SIGNIFICANT SIGN FROM THE HEAVENS

Although I was unable to go to his lecture that evening, I was told it was well attended and warmly received. However, a reporter from the *Dallas Morning News* published a critical account of his talk the next day. Although I did not read the write-up, I was told it was skeptical and cynical, and implied that Rolling Thunder was a fraud.

According to Rolling Thunder's volunteer escort, who was a friend of mine, the medicine man felt deeply embarrassed and hurt by the article. Rolling Thunder, he told me, called the reporter and told him he regretted that he harbored such negative impressions of him. In order to prove his genuineness, he told the reporter he would give him a sign later that day, one that would make clear why he was called Rolling Thunder and, he hoped, would change the reporter's mind.

Another friend of mine, who worked in air-traffic control at Love Field in Dallas, reported an extraordinary event that occurred that same afternoon while he was on duty. His comments were relayed to his wife, who worked in my medical office, and she related them to me. On this perfectly lovely, clear day, a violent storm suddenly materialized and hovered over the city. In all his years of watching weather patterns over this part of Texas, the traffic-control officer said he had never seen anything quite like it—its sudden appearance out of nowhere, its violence, its dramatic thunder, lightning, and rain, and its static localization. And suddenly it was gone. He knew he had not witnessed a typical north Texas thunderstorm.

The fact that this report came from this particular person was in itself noteworthy, because he is one of the most precise, understated, reserved, and trustworthy individuals I know. I have never known him to exaggerate *anything*. The fact that he chose even to relate this event is evidence of its singular significance. In any case, I witnessed the storm myself and was stunned by its ferocity and sudden appearance and disappearance. I knew at the time that I had experienced something highly unusual.

After his conversation with the reporter earlier that day, Rolling Thunder told my friend, his escort, that he would "make the thunder roll" to indicate his authenticity. Perhaps he had done just that. Did it change the reporter's mind? I cannot say. Was it all a mere coincidence? You decide. But if I were a skeptic, I'd think twice before tangling with a famous shaman.

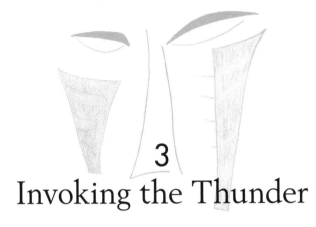

3
Invoking the Thunder

Phillip Scott

Of mixed ancestry, PHILLIP SCOTT has walked the Native Path for more than thirty years, learning from and sanctioned by traditional Medicine/Holy People, Tribal Spiritual Leaders, Wisdomkeepers, and Elders from several Indigenous cultures. He has been Sun Dancing annually in the Lakota tradition for over two decades and is a Ceremonial Leader entrusted to share Indigenous wisdom and traditional healing practices with the contemporary world. In addition to directing and teaching the programs at Ancestral Voice—Institute for Indigenous Lifeways in northern California, which he founded in 1994, he maintains a private healing practice, performs Ceremonies, gives lectures, conducts intensives, and leads pilgrimages worldwide. Having been thrice struck by Lightning (initially in 1998), he also has a close relationship with the Thunder Beings. We asked if he had ever met Rolling Thunder, and received the following reply.

MAGIC AND MAGNETISM

Circumstance never granted me an opportunity to directly encounter Rolling Thunder.

There are, however, two unique instances wherein I was privileged to experience the magic and magnetism of his Medicine.

In the late 1980s, I served as a volunteer on the Sunday shift at the Marine Mammal Center, a rescue and rehabilitation facility for injured and infirm seals, cetaceans, and otters, in northern California. Each Sunday, I faithfully awoke early in the morning to travel to the Marin Headlands to fulfill my responsibilities at the center. During one particularly sweltering summer, I rose from my bed to behold a strange and curious sight: a blustery day with torrential rains, including Thunder and Lightning. Weather phenomena such as these are an absolute rarity in the summer months, for the rains abate in the spring and the Thunder Beings hardly ever create a sound and light performance in the Bay Area—certainly not at the height of the summer season, anyway. That year was no exception. In fact, prior to that morning, we were enduring a drought.

Having an affinity for this form of weather, I relished and delighted in being buffeted by strong gusts of wind and pelted by sheets of rain while taking care of the mammals outdoors. The hospital received a report that there was a distressed pinniped (seal) down the coast, so our rescue vehicle was dispatched, another volunteer and I along with it. As a result of the gale and the sheer volume of water creating flooding in certain areas (and continuing to cascade from the Sky), navigating the roads was challenging. Arriving at our location near Santa Cruz, we encountered a formidable male California sea lion lounging on a slippery dock. As we carefully approached, he noticed our presence and with great vitality and vigor (and vocalizations) effortlessly slipped back into the water and out of our jurisdiction. Relieved that he was actually healthy, we returned to the vehicle and immediately received another report of a stranding not far from the first.

This time we were successful in our rescue mission. Once our passenger was safely secured in a carrier in the bed of the truck and we were driving back to the center along the gorgeous coast of Highway 1, the Sun emerged from the Thunderclouds, blessing us with Sun-showers, bathing the landscape in rainbows and a most breathtaking and vibrant Sunset. It was a magical, memorable, and exhilarating adventure.

The following day I spoke with a friend regarding the baffling weather and my rather remarkable experience. He reported that Rolling Thunder had visited the Bay Area and conducted a Ceremony on Saturday to invoke the Thunder Beings to bring the life-giving waters and to assist in alleviating the drought. Clearly and gratefully, his Prayers had been answered.

CONNECTING WITH THE SPIRIT OF RT

The second instance of being reached by Rolling Thunder's Medicine occurred several months after his passing. In the early 1990s, I commenced Sun Dancing on the Pine Ridge Reservation. Every summer, my Beloved wife and I would pilgrimage by automobile with others from the San Francisco Bay Area to that Rez in South Dakota. Each year, our route would take us directly past Carlin, which, to my understanding, was the city in Nevada where Rolling Thunder resided. In January 1997, unbeknownst to me that he had Journeyed Home, as we neared Carlin, I had an overwhelming impulse to connect with him. I veered off our familiar course on the interstate with the intention of directly meeting him for the first time. Having never stopped in Carlin before and without obtaining directions from locals, guided by instinct and the call of his Spirit alone, I drove directly to his home. There we were greeted and welcomed by his partner and others who informed us of the unfortunate news.

After our farewells, my supporters and I caravanned to the nearest mountain. According to RT's family and friends, RT had been fond of visiting this area. Atop the summit, my *Tiospaye* (family/community) sat in circle and I performed a *Canunpa Wakan* (Sacred Pipe) Ceremony in his honor. As I loaded the Holy Instrument of Prayer, while singing the Sacred Song that accompanies its filling, a solitary Thundercloud floated through the clear azure Sky and hovered directly overhead.

Igniting the Medicine in the bowl, while the Smoke—a visible Prayer—ascended and expanded Skyward, a gentle drizzle simultaneously descended upon us. Rolling Thunder's Blessing and presence were palpable to all in attendance.

Having fond memories of these profound experiences, I express humble gratitude to Rolling Thunder for his far-reaching Medicine—both in life as well as from the realms of Spirit.

4
Did Rolling Thunder Work at a Distance?

Bill Storm

BILL STORM is adjunct professor in the Department of Education, California State University, Sacramento. He also serves as an instrumental technology consultant for the public schools in Davis, California. After reading our previous book, *The Voice of Rolling Thunder*, Bill Storm sent Stanley a letter about a remarkable experience he had in 1983.

In 1983, after having read Doug Boyd's book about Rolling Thunder, I began paying closer attention to Indian Medicine and my relationship to the natural world. I found myself in deep gratitude for RT's teachings, and very much wished to communicate that gratitude to him. But I did not want to distract him or impose myself on his time.

As it happened, I was moving from California to New York to begin a new career, traveling by motorcycle, and my route took me past Carlin, Nevada. I bought a pound of the best pipe tobacco I could find, something I thought he might enjoy, and left it with an assistant at the front door of his home. The assistant apologized and indicated that RT was not available for visitors. But I assured him I only wished to leave the gift and was mainly grateful that I did not need to leave it on the front porch.

Traveling through the country that summer was challenging given that there were multiple thunderstorms accompanying my trip. Almost every day I encountered violent weather—not ideal when someone is riding a motorcycle. On my first day after leaving Carlin, as the first storm loomed ahead of me, I stopped to put on my rain suit. But while wearing my rain suit in the day's humidity, my motorcycle and I did not get wet. The rain did not fall on me. The suit and I both remained quite dry. I was glad for my "good luck."

On the second day, the same thing happened. I rode underneath thick black clouds and the rain fell behind me. It also fell—and hailed—ahead of me, but I continued to ride under a rainless sky. The road was wet with rain that had fallen just ahead.

ROLLING THUNDER'S ROLLING DRY SPOT

For six days as I traveled and camped the rain fell, often in torrents, but not once did it fall on me as I rode. I recall arriving at a campground somewhere in the Midwest, the rain starting to fall only after I had made it to the campsite, parked, and put up my tent.

By the end of my "rolling dry spot," I knew Rolling Thunder had been at work on my behalf, and I understood that my good fortune was no coincidence. It was as if RT had surrounded me with a special relationship to the sky. I began to feel the phenomenon he had arranged.

It is only recently, as I entered my sixties, that I have grown to understand the nature of the relationship RT had forged with the universe. It has taken me this long to find my way, thanks to a meditation practice granting me access to a clear path. I wrote this to add yet another story to the wonderful life that was Rolling Thunder's. I never met the man, but he is for me someone like my own grandfather, whom

I did not know well before he passed, but whom I came to appreciate as I grew into maturity.

Thank you, Stanley and Sidian, for the book I now enjoy. I am grateful to you both, as I always have been to Rolling Thunder for that dry ride so many years ago.

5
Is Rolling Thunder Still Having Fun?

Karel James Bouse

KAREL JAMES BOUSE is a teacher, theatrical artist, and shamanic practitioner. As well, she is a doctoral candidate in psychology at Saybrook University. In 2014, she wrote us a provocative letter about an experience related to Rolling Thunder.

Please allow me to preface this anecdote with a few sentences about my relationship with altered-consciousness states and the possible inhabitants of both other levels of reality and also where I live. This is simply to help the reader put my account of my experience with Rolling Thunder in context.

My ancestry is predominantly Welsh, and my family hails from the South Carolina upstate. The upstate is a unique cultural matrix that holds the supernatural beliefs and shamanic/hoodoo customs of the Welsh Diaspora—that emigrated to South Carolina in the seventeenth century—plus the Cherokee, and finally the influence of people from Africa and the Caribbean. The unseen is part of life, and in the upstate we grow up with an understanding that fairies, animal spirits, haints (ghosts), and other powerful nature entities are real. I have lived in east Tennessee, which shares much of the same beliefs in the preternatural as the South Carolina upstate, for twenty-two years. I currently make my home in a wooded area next door to a Cherokee burial mound. The Smoky Mountains are visible to the east and south, and Tellico Lake is a block from our backyard. Visits from eagles, hawks, osprey, and deer are frequent, and we share our property with some fearless squirrels, migrating birds, and a tribe of crows. It is a very special place indeed.

"IS ROLLING THUNDER FOR REAL?"

I read *The Voice of Rolling Thunder* by Stanley Krippner and Sidian Morning Star Jones in the late autumn of 2013. I had purchased the book from Dr. Krippner at Saybrook University's August conference in San Francisco, and he kindly sent me a personally autographed copy. The book became my preferred bedtime reading in mid-November, and I finally finished it just before turning out the light at around 10:30 p.m. on December 7, 2013. I had read the book with a very open mind and a great deal of interest, but with the lingering question as to the nature of Rolling Thunder himself. Was he the remarkable shape-shifting healer who distorted the time-space continuum at will to gather herbs a hundred miles away? Or was he a charismatic individual with healing gifts who was as much snake oil as he was true medicine? Having met a few self-aggrandizing and self-proclaimed "miracle workers" in my time, it is understandable that despite my inclination and desire to believe everything that I was reading about RT in the book, I could not completely quench a healthy dose of skepticism. I recall that my last thought that night before going to sleep was "I wonder if he was real?"

The answer to my question was not long in coming. Sometime during the wee hours of the morning I snapped awake out of a sound sleep. Lying in bed I could see through the windows into the woods in front of our house. Suddenly there was a brilliant purple-white flash of forked lightning that illuminated the bare trees outside the window. That flash awakened me completely! The weather had been clear; there were no storms anywhere around the region. The temperatures were typical for southeast Tennessee in early December (in the upper 50s for highs and overnight lows in the upper 30s). These were not conditions conducive to the development of thunderstorms.

Immediately I began counting off the seconds between the lightning and the sound of thunder to determine how far away the storm was. When I had reached eighteen seconds, there was a crashing thud that sounded like someone dropping a bowling ball on a hard wooden floor—and then it began to roll. Indeed, it rolled toward us from the west to the east. As it rolled it rumbled, and as it came closer, the ground and the trees and the house began to shake. The windows rattled, the walls trembled, and the furnishings and wall hangings rattled. In fact, everything in the house was shaking.

My husband woke up and asked me to stop whatever it was I was doing: but I was doing *nothing*. The thunder rolled not over but through our house, (which is about seventy-eight feet long), from the bedroom down the hallway, through the kitchen, and finally through the family room until exiting over the Indian mound and moving out to the lake.

Then all was quiet.

The next morning we checked online to see if there had been any reports of odd weather phenomena in the area (there were none) or whether the United States Geodetic Survey had recorded a quake anywhere in the area (again there was nothing). It would seem that what we had experienced was an anomalous event that did not originate from so-called natural causes. Although I am very sensitive to thunderstorms (having been born in one) this did not feel like a "normal" thunderstorm.

I have no idea why RT's spirit would care one way or the other whether a woman in Tennessee believed in his authenticity, but this sequence of events might indicate that, if nothing else, he decided to have some fun. If it was RT he certainly made his point. If it wasn't RT, then it was likely our friendly neighbors from the mound having a great party!

PART 2

Thunder Healing

When it comes to medicine, nobody has a monopoly on knowledge.

ROLLING THUNDER

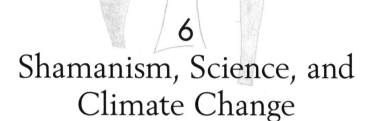

6
Shamanism, Science, and Climate Change

Stephan A. Schwartz

STEPHAN A. SCHWARTZ is a Distinguished Consulting Faculty Member of Saybrook University and a research associate of the Cognitive Sciences Laboratory of the Laboratories for Fundamental Research. He is the columnist for the journal *Explore: The Journal of Science and Healing*, and editor of the daily Web publication *Schwartzreport.net*, covering trends that are affecting the future. Stephen is the author of several books, including *The 8 Laws of Change*. At our request, he wrote the following reflection about his encounter with RT and how it impacted his life.

Early one high summer evening in Virginia Beach, Virginia, during the late 1960s, I spent time with Shoshone medicine man Rolling Thunder and helped him set up a healing ceremony. It involved two teenage boys, both with serious, unhealed wounds. Along with about fifty other people, a large percentage of whom were physicians, I stood in the mostly unpaved parking lot behind the lecture hall of the

Association for Research and Enlightenment, the organization whose nexus was the work of Edgar Cayce. We were gathered in a circle around a massage table and watched as a boy was brought out on a rolling gurney from an ambulance and laid upon the table. The dressing on his legs had been taken off, and it was easy to see he had a serious wound that went deep into the muscle. I had seen such wounds as a medic in the army.

Holding the breast and extended wing of a crow, Rolling Thunder made stroking movements over the boy's leg. At the end of each pass, he flicked the wing toward a piece of steak that lay on the ground at the head of the table. I understood that the crow wing was a healing totem consistent with Rolling Thunder's Native American healing tradition. That was singular, but it was what happened next that changed my world view in several ways. As he made those passes, others and I saw a mist form around Rolling Thunder's body in the summer twilight, extending out from his body by about six to eighteen inches. It grew in intensity as his hand with the crow's wing moved over the boy's wound. It was mesmerizing and, when Rolling Thunder was finished and had stepped back from the table, we could see that the boy's large open wound had closed. Not only that, but it looked as one's skin does when the scab comes off: taut, smooth, and pink. It defied what any of us doctors or laymen understood about the human body, but it could not be denied (Schwartz 2012, 41).

At the time, I was only beginning to study consciousness research, and had just begun daily meditation. I took what I had seen for what it so obviously was: a genuine consciousness phenomenon brought about through a shamanic technique. The doctors who were present told me that it was clear that no magic trick could explain it.

After it was over I stood in the parking lot, staring at the empty massage table, replaying in my mind what had happened. Just then I noticed that the steak on the ground was withered, as if decayed. Since I had bought that porterhouse and it had just come out of the cooler, I had no idea what could have done that to it.

SEEING IS BELIEVING

To determine what others thought, I entered into conversation with them; it was very interesting to hear what the physicians had to say. Far better trained about the healing processes of the human body than I was, they came at it with a more expert eye. And what they saw was very disconcerting. They knew from the workup of the attending physician, which had been made available, what the boy's condition was, and what had been tried. What they had just witnessed did not accord with any of that, and it made a number of them very agitated. One could say that they experienced "reality vertigo"—confronting an undeniable experience that should not be possible.

At a personal level the experience played a significant role in my own decision to study the nature of consciousness, including the process of therapeutic intention, what most would call healing. It also channeled my interest through an anthropological lens. I am the last living founder of the Society for the Anthropology of Consciousness of the American Anthropological Association. It is largely because of what I witnessed that evening that throughout my career I have pursued parallel lines of research: experimental science and a cross-cultural study of shamanic, religious, and spiritual traditions, paying particular attention to where they and objective science converge.

I go into all this because I think the same world that came to understand that level of healing might have something else to say to which we ought to listen. The world of Rolling Thunder is an ancient one of empirical wisdom, developed and refined through years and generations of close observation and passed down through ritual, apprenticeship, and experience. If Rolling Thunder had a hero, it was the nineteenth-century Nez Perce leader Chief Joseph, the brilliant tactician who outmaneuvered one of the great battle generals of the U.S. Army general William Tecumseh Sherman. For Chief Joseph the world was a single living unity. Even artfully retreating from pursuing cavalry, he was observed to stop and get off his horse to "inspect and smell a flower that was new to him" (Schwartz 2012, 41). Rolling Thunder mirrored these sentiments, and when he began to have considerable contact with the non-Native American world, often asked the psychologists and physicians he had come to know why it was that the ongoing destruction of the Earth was not seen as a psychiatric disorder? He saw the exploitative materialistic world view as a form of mental illness. And he had a rather bleak view of the future because of the growing imbalances—to which he was witness—in the great systems of nature as a result of exploitation and pollution.

In the generation before Chief Joseph, there had been Chief Si'ahl (Seattle), a chief of the Duwamish tribe whose ancestral homelands are, in part, where the city of Seattle exists today. In 1854 he was recorded as saying, "Humankind has not woven the web of life. We are but one thread within it. Whatever we do to the web, we do to ourselves. All things are bound together. All things connect" (Chief Seattle, *California Indian Education*).

CONSCIOUSNESS IS FUNDAMENTAL

This same indigenous sense of the web of life is not particular to North American tribal cultures. In South America, the Kogi (meaning "jaguar"), are an indigenous people who live in an unusually remote and isolated mountain range that runs through the Sierra Nevada de Santa Marta. The Sierra Nevada is the world's highest coastal mountain range. The Kogi quite consciously choose to remain apart from the general Colombian culture. They believe that one of the mountains in the range, Pico Cristóbal Colón, is "the Heart of the World" and that they are the "Elder Brother" and we, the others outside their culture, are the "Younger Brother."

To guide their culture the Kogi have developed a shamanic nonlocal consciousness corps called Mamas. The Kogi identify a small number of male children at birth and put them in a cave system where they spend the first nine years of their lives attended only by their mother and the priests. They are taught deep meditation and focusing techniques, which open them to nonlocal consciousness, which they characterize as a Great Mother they call Aluna. It is a system not unlike the temple attendants at the Delphic Oracle in Greece, the Talking Idol of Sihwa in Egypt (a specially trained temple attendant that spoke through a physical idol), or the conceptually similar Mayan Oracle of Ix Chel on the Mexican island of Cozumel. When they are brought out of the cave and introduced into the larger culture, their role is to remain open to the nonlocal and to report what they see about the future, or individuals, or the community.

Like Rolling Thunder, Chiefs Joseph and Seattle, and many other North American shamans, the Mamas of the Kogi see Earth as a living network, one in which consciousness is fundamental, and physical reality, space-time, is its manifestation. By 1990, just as the first scientific papers about climate change were coming out, the Mamas had become so concerned about what "Younger Brother" was doing to the planet that they broke their isolation and reached out. Alan Erira, a BBC documentarian, was given unique access to the Kogi, and the result was the documentary *The Heart of the World: Elder Brother's Warning.* If you have not seen it, I recommend that you do so

The aborigines of Australia tell a similar story and have similar concerns. What is interesting about these paths is that although they arise in many geographical areas and have different cultural symbols, they have a common world view: Behind the physical world is a domain of consciousness. This is a matrix of life interconnected and interdependent, an interactive world where the individual is both informing of and informed by this domain of consciousness. In this world view, humanity does not live independent of the world, in dominion over it, but is enmeshed in the matrix. Although couched in symbols that have been largely made clichés as the result of Caucasian co-option, conceptually it is a very sophisticated world view in which consciousness is primary.

Such views are oppositional to the materialist science model. In that world view the consciousness of each individual is isolated within their physiology. Earth is seen as a dead resource to plunder or dominate. Consciousness has no real role. Gilbert Ryle, Waynflete Professor of Metaphysical Philosophy at Oxford, coined a term, *the ghost in the machine,* in his book *The Concept of the Mind,* as a way of criticizing Descartes' mind-body dualism, which he saw as absurd. Since then the nature of consciousness has been largely explored, but only from the assumption that it was, as of yet, understood to be a neurophysiologic process entirely resident in the organism. Its inherent physicality became an ironbound axiom. However, a growing body of experimental research now challenges this, reflecting a view much more aligned with that of Chief Seattle, Chief Joseph, and Rolling Thunder.

Science is always about change, but rarely about a change in paradigm. But such a change is now underway in science. Still a minority position, it is nonetheless the trend direction in a wide range of disciplines, from medicine to biology to physics. Whole new subdisciplines have emerged, driven by the results of this research despite Ryle's dismissive words. This work is pushing toward a new paradigm, one that is neither dualist nor monist, but rather postulates that consciousness is the fundamental basis of reality. Max Planck, the father of quantum mechanics, framed it very clearly in an interview with the respected British newspaper *The Observer* in its January 25, 1931, edition. Context is always important, and Planck understood very well that he was taking a public position, speaking as one of the leading physicists of his generation, through one of Britain's most important papers. He did not mince words: "I regard consciousness as fundamental. I regard matter as derivative from consciousness. We cannot get behind consciousness. Everything that we talk about, everything that we regard as existing, postulates consciousness."

For Sir Martin Rees, Astronomer Royal of England, it looks this way, "In the beginning there were only probabilities. The universe could only come into existence if someone observed it. It does not matter that the observers turned up several billion years later. The universe exists because we are aware of it" (Rees 2006, 193).

Science and shamanism have converged. Science now tells us, as the indigenous world view has been saying for millennia, that we don't live on the Earth, we live *in* the Earth, centered in a cocoon that extends several miles below its surface. Worms have been found several miles deep into mines, and in 2013, were found 6.8 miles (11 kilometers) into Earth's crust at the bottom of the sea (Yong 2014). And far above us spacecraft experience atmospheric effects beginning 75 miles out (120 kilometers). Beyond that lie the protective veils of the magnetosphere. Just as the empirical wisdom of ancient people describe, we are embedded in a vast interlocking system in which consciousness plays a powerful role. From the perspective of this matrix, wellness at every level, from individual to planetary, suddenly becomes the most desirable state and of primary importance. At this point both science and shamanism are of one mind.

So it is worth looking at Rolling Thunder's vision for the future and seeing how it and Western science compare. Friends who spoke with him recall him saying, "Rolling Thunder frequently pointed out that the sickness of the natural environment is a reflection of the sickness of human beings. That Europeans exploited Nature rather than working with Nature" (Jones and Krippner 2012, 266).

NEARING THE TIPPING POINT

In early June 2012, a group of scientists who had each spent years studying Earth's biosphere from many different aspects felt compelled to come forward with a very clear warning: All the life forms on Earth faced a human-created planet-wide tipping point whose consequences would be difficult at best, but catastrophic without adequate preparation and mitigation. Their paper in *Nature* (Barnosky 2012, 52) said: "Localized ecological systems are known to shift abruptly and irreversibly from one state to another when they are forced across critical thresholds. Here we review evidence that the global ecosystem as a whole can react in the same way and is approaching a planetary-scale critical transition as a result of human influence."

A confluence of trends: overpopulation, the continuing destruction of both terrestrial and marine ecosystems, and climate change—they are described as all interlinked—are creating a world very different from the one in which we live today and the epoch in which recorded human history has taken place, eighteenth-century mini ice age and all.

"It really will be a new world, biologically, at that point," warns Anthony Barnosky, professor of Integrative Biology at the University of California, Berkeley, and lead author.

> The data suggests that there will be a reduction in biodiversity and severe impacts on much of what we depend on to sustain our quality of life, including, for example, fisheries, agriculture, forest products and clean water. This could happen within just a few generations. My view is that humanity is at a crossroads now, where we have to make an active choice. One choice is to acknowledge these issues and potential consequences and try to guide the future . . . or throw up our hands and say, "Let's just go on as usual and see what happens." My guess is, if we take that latter choice, yes, humanity is going to survive, but we are going to see effects that will seriously degrade the quality of life for our children and grandchildren (Sanders 2012).

And the day after the Barnosky et al. paper was published, the National Oceanic and Atmospheric Administration issued a report saying that the period of March through May 2012 was the warmest it had been in the contiguous United States since record keeping began in 1895 ("State of the Climate" 2012).

The 2014 climate report from the Intergovernmental Panel of Climate Change (IPCC) made our situation very clear: Climate change is almost entirely due to human culture. It's our fault, and we may have to reduce greenhouse gas emissions to zero by the end of this century if we are to preserve something resembling the civilization we now have (Intergovernmental Panel on Climate Change. *Climate Change 2014 Synthesis Report*).

In October of that year, Rajendra K. Pachauri, Chairman of the IPCC, said to the opening session of the fortieth meeting of the IPCC:

> Much has been made of the growing peril of delaying the hard choices that need to be made to adapt to and mitigate climate change. I do not discount those challenges. But the Synthesis Report shows that solutions are at hand. Tremendous strides are being made in alternative sources of clean energy. There is much we can do to use energy more efficiently. Reducing and ultimately eliminating deforestation provides additional avenues for action. This is not to say it will be easy. It won't. A great deal of work and tall hurdles lie ahead. But it can be done. We still have time to build a better, more sustainable world. We still have time to avoid the most serious impacts of climate change. But we have precious little of that time (Pachauri 2014).

In the world of climate change the only remediation is to change those behaviors that are creating the problem—or die. As *Science Daily* reported ("Social Scientists Build Case . . ." 2009), "In a wide range of studies, social scientists are amassing a growing body of evidence to show we are evolving to become more compassionate and collaborative in our quest to survive and thrive."

Psychologist Dacher Keltner, codirector of UC Berkeley's Greater Good Science Center, explains it this way: "Because of our very vulnerable offspring, the fundamental task for human survival and gene replication is to take care of others. Human beings have survived as a species because we have evolved the capacities to care for those in need and to cooperate. As Darwin long ago surmised, sympathy is our strongest instinct."

Rolling Thunder and the tradition from which he arose have been trying to teach us lessons that we finally are beginning to hear. We live in a matrix of life and we must do all we can to protect it. In the words of Chief Seattle, "Take only memories, leave nothing but footprints." We must learn to live by these words if we, the planet, and all its creatures are to survive.

7

An Exorcism in California

Jean Millay, Ph.D.

JEAN MILLAY, PH.D., is a writer, graphic artist, prize-winning filmmaker, psychical researcher, and pioneer in the use of biofeedback in education. Her doctoral dissertation centered on a pioneering experiment in which telepathy was attempted between pairs of intimate friends whose brain waves were being monitored. She is the author of *Multidimensional Mind* and the editor/author of *Silver Threads: 25 Years of Parapsychology Research* and *Radiant Minds: Scientists Explore the Dimensions of Consciousness*. It was at a party she held for the tabla virtuoso Allah Rakha that Stanley Krippner met Mickey Hart, a member of the fabled Grateful Dead rock band. Later, Mickey introduced Stanley to Rolling Thunder. Hence, Jean Millay is partly responsible for the publication of this book.

The first time I met Rolling Thunder, I was surprised. I had read about his power as a Native American medicine man in Doug Boyd's 1974 book, *Rolling Thunder,* and I was expecting to see a dark-skinned Native. I spent some early years on a ranch in Wabuska, Nevada, where Piute Indians lived around us, and some helped with the harvest. One wonderful woman named Suzy came to help my grandmother feed the crew during that time. Suzy would just show up with her suitcase and say simply, "You need me; I come now." She even made a papoose basket for my doll, and we all loved her.

One particularly memorable experience occurred when my sisters and I were walking home from school. It started to rain a few big drops, so we ran into the granary, which was mostly empty, and listened to the rain on the metal roof, waiting for it to pass. As we opened the door to enter the granary, there in the center of this round room sat Suzy on her bedroll in full yoga position, eyes open but not seeming to see us. What a shock! We hadn't known she was at the ranch, and her manner was so strange to us that we apologized and, backing out, closed the door, leaving her in peace. This was the first time I had ever seen anyone in a trance. Nor did I know what a trance was. Mother explained to us that some Native Americans seemed to use telepathic powers, which is why Suzy always knew when she was needed to help feed the crew. None of us had telephones way out on the ranch in those days.

My friend Stanley Krippner needed a ride to a warehouse-type building that the rock band the Grateful Dead used for practice. He said that Rolling Thunder would be there, and by then I wanted to meet this powerful medicine man. We arrived at the rehearsal space and people were milling around in the low light. As I looked around, I didn't see anyone who fit my image of what Rolling Thunder might look like. Eventually I saw a light-skinned man with a strong aura and a feather in his hat. *That must be him,* I thought, and shortly thereafter Stan introduced us.

RT had just finished working on *Billy Jack,* the movie based, in part, on his life. I had not seen the film, but when we were introduced, he commented that my name (Jean) was the same as that of the lead woman in the film. He looked at me very carefully, and I felt that although he might be a spiritual medicine man, he was, at that first meeting, sizing me up with his eyes, the way a man sizes up a woman. *Hmmmm.* Well, I *did* want to know more about how a medicine man comprehended healing, but I would have to be very wary of him also. I mean, besides being a compelling medicine man, he was at the core a lusty fellow.

THE YOGI INCIDENT

As it turned out, I didn't see RT again until I was at the Westerbeke Ranch in Sonoma County for a meeting. I was still living in the Sacramento area at the time, and drove down to Sonoma to attend the meeting. By this time, I was feeling weird, and friends told me I looked as though I had a dark cloud over my head. I was sure I was suffering from a hex. I had experienced a negative interaction with a yogi from India. I wasn't one of his students but a friend was, and I felt he was using his position as her "teacher" to persuade her to give him some property she owned in New York for an ashram he wanted to build there. I had encouraged her to refuse, thus invoking the yogi's ire.

A year or so earlier, I had joined a spiritual healing circle conducted weekly by a gentle woman who previously had been affiliated with a church in a different state. One of our healing-circle members was a Christian minister. He said he would be willing to do an exorcism for me if I came to his church for the ceremony. Even then, I was much more interested in shamanism than in Christianity, but I agreed to his terms. He was very kind, and afterward I did feel some release.

However, a year or so later, the students of this same hotshot yogi wanted him to become affiliated with the Humanistic Psychology Institute.*

A problem arose, however, when the students of this yogi threatened to file a lawsuit against the Humanistic Psychology Institute (HPI). The yogi wanted to meet directly with Stan to discuss the problem; however, he would not come to the HPI office. Instead, he insisted

---

*The current name is Saybrook University.

that he and Stan meet at an ashram in San Francisco where he was still held in high regard. Stan acquiesced to this meeting, after which he was due to catch a flight out of California. When I learned he needed a ride to meet with the yogi as well as to the airport, I told him I would give him a lift.

Stan and I then arrived at the ashram, where the yogi kept him waiting for nearly an hour, even though he knew that Stan needed to catch a plane. When the yogi finally appeared, he said he was late because he had been doing some healing at a hospital. He was dressed in a long white robe that looked as though it was made out of upholstery material. I told Stan, "This character expects to be treated as a spiritual teacher. If you do so, he will reveal his mind to you. But whatever he says to you, don't get angry. He has arranged this meeting in a room next to the place where all of his students are eating, and they will be able to hear any raised voice."

Stan understood this and kept his temper. As I advised, he treated the yogi with deference, even though the yogi had made some threatening comments to Stan. Their private meeting was over with barely enough time left to spare for me to get Stan to the airport on time for his flight. This face-to-face meeting was enough to show Stan that this man did not act like a spiritual teacher. However, in the meeting, Stan apologized for any lack of respect that had been paid him, and the yogi's students backed off on his request to become affiliated with the institute.

After that stressful interaction, I again felt as though a black cloud hung over my head. Shortly thereafter, RT came to Sonoma State College* to give a talk, which was not very well organized, but was rather a rambling series of fascinating stories. After that event, he went out to the Westerbeke Ranch, where he and his family of helpers were staying, to give another talk. I wondered if he might do an exorcism on me. I waited for a quiet moment and then I approached him to ask him

---

*Its current name is Sonoma State University.

about this and was delighted when he granted my request.

Suddenly, the rambling storyteller turned into something else. His eyes became more intense. He ignored the crowd of people in the background. He did not flirt with me, but became very serious. He pulled out his eagle feather, mumbled a few words silently, and spit on his hand. I suddenly felt as if a fifty-pound weight had been lifted from my shoulders.

I still remember this amazing change in him. It was as if he had turned into a completely different person before my very eyes. And I know *I* did, for the exorcism was successful and I was never troubled by that black cloud again.

8
An Exorcism in Wyoming

John Perry Barlow

JOHN PERRY BARLOW is the cofounder of the Electronic Frontier Foundation and executive vice president of Algae Systems. He is a fellow of Harvard University's Berkman Center for Internet and Society and a retired Wyoming cattle rancher and political activist. He is a childhood friend of Bob Weir of the Grateful Dead, and wrote lyrics for the band for several years. In 2014, he and Stanley spoke at San Jose University as part of a program sponsored by the Grateful Dead Scholars. This encounter led him to reminiscence about his contact with RT.

Whenever I found myself near Carlin, Nevada, I would drop by Rolling Thunder's home and pay him and his family a visit. He never greeted me with a great deal of enthusiasm, but that was not his style. His way of greeting guests was more muted and he did not make a big fuss about visitors. However, I knew I was welcome because he treated me just as if I had been there all along and had never left.

I had first met RT through Bobby Weir and the Grateful Dead. In January 1972, Bobby and I were spending the night in a homestead cabin in rural Nevada, a structure that had seen better days and was just barely livable. It was part of a cattle ranch that had long since been deserted. This cabin had a reputation for being haunted but we paid little attention to that because it was hotter than hell that night and we just hoped we could get some sleep.

ROLLING THUNDER AS GHOSTBUSTER

About three o'clock in the morning I heard some commotion upstairs. The cause of it, apparently, was a ghost that Bobby was convinced he'd seen. Worse yet, the ghost would not let him get to sleep. Bobby insisted on phoning RT, even though it was the middle of the night. When he told RT about the ghost, RT did not seem upset about being awakened because he took things like ghosts very seriously. He told Bobby that Bobby needed to exorcise the ghost. He gave Bobby specific directions, sort of a do-it-yourself exorcism.

RT said the first thing to do was to take an old coffee can and punch holes in the side. This would be the container for some substances that would need to be burned. Second, RT said that Bobby should find a cedar tree and take several strips of bark from it because they would be needed for the exorcism. But Bobby never allowed RT to go on to the next step because Bobby wanted instantaneous results.

RT was uncommonly patient with Bobby and gave him another set of instructions. RT asked Bobby if he had a set of Strike Anywhere matches, the type that work regardless of the temperature or the weather. Bobby replied that he usually carried a box of those same matches with him. RT was happy to hear that news. RT told Bobby to light every match in the box. Then he would need to take a knife handle and grind the burned match heads into a powder. Finally, he needed to cover his face with the ashes. The ghost would take one look at the results and would disappear.

This must have worked because Bobby was able to get back to sleep. The next morning I woke up at about six and walked upstairs to where Bobby was sleeping. I knocked on the door. When there was no response, I let myself in. I saw Bobby asleep in bed, but he was unrecognizable. His face was completely black, just as if he were a character in an old-fashioned minstrel show, or he was Al Jolson singing in blackface in his movie *The Jazz Singer.*

I hollered, "What the hell is going on?"

This woke up Bobby and he told me the whole story.

So now we both knew how to scare away ghosts. And we realized that RT had a remedy for just about everything.

9

A Recurring Dream

Brian Wilkes

BRIAN WILKES is a journalist, educator, and prolific author. A descendant of the Croatan people of North Carolina, he is active with efforts to teach and preserve the Cherokee language, and is part of the prestigious Cherokee Bible Project. He is a minister in the Native American Church of Nemenhah, which is based in Stockton, Missouri, and a doctoral candidate working with other indigenous healers. He lives in southern Illinois. When he heard that we were writing a second book about Rolling Thunder, he was eager to make this contribution.

It was 1993. I had the dream again. It had been recurring for months.

I was driving west along Interstate 80, which was just two miles from my New Jersey home. I drove west, through the Plains, and into the Rockies. Where was I going? I was a writer and two publishers who often bought my work were in the Los Angeles area. Maybe I was going to see them, although my dream was unclear about my destination.

But I never reached California. Somewhere in the twists and turns of the Rockies, my path always ended. Nevertheless, here were people who seemed to know me and were expecting me, like family I had never met. Maybe I had reservations at a campground?

Where was I going, and why?

The phone startled me back to waking consciousness. Had I known then the events this call would set in motion, I might never have answered it.

"Is this Brian Wilkes?" the gruff voice demanded.

I admitted it was, wondering who now had my unlisted number.

"This is Rolling Thunder in Nevada. I hear you have some questions."

"Some questions!" Now *that* was an understatement, if I'd ever heard one!

Rolling Thunder was a well-known Cherokee healer who had broken with tradition back in the 1960s by accepting non-Native students. That just wasn't done—but neither was calling somebody out of the blue, asking whether or not they had any questions. He had been the role model for the 1971 cult film *Billy Jack,* and just a few days earlier I had finished reading Doug Boyd's 1976 account of his travels with the medicine man.

But how did Rolling Thunder know all that?

There was something in the voice that told me this was someone who was accustomed to getting straight answers.

I did have questions, but where to start?

Why had my family been so reluctant to discuss our Native ancestry, speaking of it only obliquely, if ever? Why was Cherokee tradition and language so different from the cultures that surrounded it? What had happened to the majority of the Cherokee mixed-blood people who scattered to the winds at the time of the Removal and the Trail of Tears? Was this current world cycle really going to end in a cataclysm as Cherokee prophecies foretold? Why did I have these strange waking dreams? And the real killer, What was I supposed to do about any of this, if anything? (And, by the way, how did you get my unlisted phone number? Never mind, maybe I don't want to know.)

In the next few months, I'd have a few of these questions answered but many new ones were raised. I'd learn to leave a window open before lighting cedar in a haunted building. I'd learn to leave an offering before picking any wild plant. I'd learn how RT used his "cranky old man" mask to test his would-be students.

In the next few years, I'd learn that traditional Elders seldom ask a question unless they already know the answer, so don't bother bluffing. They aren't asking for information or testing your knowledge; they're testing your integrity.

And I'd learn to expect phone calls from RT, wherein he would ask me about something that had just happened in my life moments before, or congratulate me on the way I had handled the incident. I'd lose and regain my faith in my Creator, my people, humanity in general, and myself—several times. I would be there as eagle feathers and tobacco pouches moved through space and time, driving scientific instruments crazy. And I would be attacked by just about everyone at one time or another, even subjected to death threats, while developing the proverbial hide seven layers thick expected of leaders and exemplars.

I'd lose Rolling Thunder in 1997, never having had the chance to meet him face-to-face, but I'd regain him again as other Elders in distant lands described the "teacher" who was standing by me, or who was giving them instructions to relay to me. I would also learn that Rolling Thunder had lived for years in the high plateau of Nevada, right there in Carlin on Interstate 80, where I had driven so many times in my dreams.

A CALLING FROM PERU

In the spring of 1998 a group of Quechua Elders in Lima, Peru, invited me down to participate in the dedication of a community center, which would include the enactment of various ceremonial rituals. The ten-year civil war had driven many indigenous people from the mountains into the cities, where they didn't fit. Looking around for an example of Native people who had adapted to the modern world without losing their own culture, they settled upon the Cherokee. They wanted to meet with me because of my knowledge of the Cherokee nations and because I could teach them the Cherokee language.

As I prepared for the trip, rumors started coming back from Cherokees around the country whom I had sought out for advice. There was more than meets the eye in the connection between Cherokees and Peruvian Natives, I was told. Sequoyah, who had created the Cherokee writing system, died in 1843 on a trip to Mexico while seeking a reported community of Cherokees who had settled there years earlier. Another source in North Carolina told me that Sequoyah had actually been on his way to Cuzco, the old Incan capital, to deposit items or records for safekeeping. Fabulous legends of this kind abound in Native America, and some of the most outlandish tales eventually prove to have some basis in truth. You can't discount them out of hand.

It was at this point that one of the seers sent a strange message: "Don't touch the water before doing the ceremonial purifications." I wasn't sure what this meant. On one level it could have been a warning against amoebic dysentery. But when I asked who had sent the message, the seer said, "RT." It had been just about a year since Rolling Thunder had passed.

Okay, I thought. RT might well be sending messages, but I didn't know what water he was talking about, although I did know that the community center we would be dedicating was someplace close to the ocean.

I e-mailed this concern about the water to my contacts in Peru, without mentioning the source of the comment.

The word came back in a few days. "Yes, we know the water he means. We'll go there first." Any attempt to extract further details or even our destination proved to be relatively fruitless, although I did learn that the water in question was a lake.

"Which lake?"

"A sacred lake."

Further inquiries brought only "a *very* sacred lake."

When we arrived in Lima, our host Sergio took us to his home, where we met Don Enrique, a man who appeared to be in his forties and who, I would soon learn, was a highly regarded spiritual leader of the mountain communities who were then refugees in Lima. He looked at me strangely for a few minutes, then made a gesture like a raptor's claw. "You did a ceremony recently," he said through interpreters. "You used a claw against a dark creature."

I indeed had used an eagle claw to drive off a vampirelike creature that had been tormenting a friend, but I had not spoken of it to anyone.

"You put your claw into it," the Elder continued, "but you don't realize it also put its claw into you, and left a poison that is heading for your heart. Unless we act soon, it will kill you in a few days." These words alarmed me but I was helpless to do anything about them, except follow the old man's directives.

"In the morning," said our host, "we will set out for the sacred lake."

A HEART-STOPPING MOMENT

Three hundred miles north of Lima sits Huascarán National Park, named for the highest peak in the Cordillera Blanca (22,199 feet/ 6,768 meters). The climate in the park ranges from subtropical at its lowest level to subarctic at its height. It was here that we arrived the next day, after many hours of vertical and horizontal travel. Specifically, we arrived at Lagunas Llanganuco, a pair of glacial and geothermal lakes at the base of Peru's tallest mountain. Since it was late, we went to bed.

After a few hours of sleep, I was awakened by Don Enrique, who was speaking in a rapid, agitated manner. He tried to slow down so I could understand him, but the only words I could make out were *amarillo intenso*—"intense yellow."

Accepting the futility of teaching me instant Spanish, he left, only to return with Sergio, his translator, who was already awake and dressed.

Sergio translated Enrique's words: "He says a spirit came to awaken him, to give him a vision. He doesn't know this spirit, but it's your teacher."

With that, Enrique interjected *"tu maestro"* ("your teacher").

"You will understand this soon," Sergio told me, translating again for Enrique.

On foot we went to the edge of one of the lakes, where Don Enrique asked me to proceed with my ceremony. Rolling Thunder had taught me that one of the first protocols was never to make ceremony on someone else's land without obtaining their permission first. One must also be introduced to the local spirits and ancestors. At each step of the procedure, I told Don Enrique what I intended to do, and asked if that was acceptable to him and to the local spirits. He would nod silently. I offered medicine plants and a large gemstone as gifts to the spirits who resided in the lakes and the mountains.

"What else would you do?" he asked, when I had paused for a moment.

"I would enter the water and pour it over my head seven times."

He nodded.

I stood in shin-deep water not far from the shore. As I poured water over my head the seventh time, the scene began to change, and images began to weave in and out before me, as if I were switching channels on a TV. For a long moment I could no longer tell which way led back to shore before the voices of my companions pierced my awareness, becoming a beacon guiding me back to them. However, when I reached them, I realized I had no heartbeat, no pulse. Instead, all was deafening silence. I slumped against one of them and said, "My heart has stopped."

Enrique sprang up and said that he had to take me back into the water. We stood together in shallow water, and he drew two small stones from his pouch and held them against my rib cage. With this and a jolt, my heart suddenly lurched back to life.

THE APUS OF THE MOUNTAIN

After the shock of all of this had passed, Enrique and I sat down on the shore and he explained that the area we were in was considered the home of the strongest Apus, or residing spirits of the mountain. They were addressed simply as Apu Huascaran and Apu Huandoy. Don Enrique went on to say that when a person sets foot on property that the Apus oversee, the Apus will examine the heart of that person, make a determination about him, and then decide how to interact with him.

The Apus of this particular locale had a reputation for not tolerating pretension. Don Enrique told of a shaman from northern Peru who had come to Huascarán a few years earlier with an entourage of his followers, and didn't think he needed to ask one of the local *curanderos* for a formal introduction to the Apus. According to Don Enrique, this shaman had been struck dead next to the lake. (Like much of the high Andes, this region is known for *charki rayo*, "dry lightning," which may come without warning from a cloudless sky.)

Those who have entered the lake, which is unexpectedly warm (suggesting geothermal heating) and opaque turquoise in color (suggesting the presence of copper and other minerals), attest to its disorienting effects. "Had these disorienting effects been partially or wholly responsible for what happened to me?" I asked Enrique.

"You have had a heart defect since childhood," he replied. "The dark creature was able to use that. The spirits of this place decided that while you have much to learn, you have come here with good intention, and you have been taught proper respect. So they decided that you should live and that you should receive the teachings. And they desired to heal you, but to do this, they had to stop your heart so that it could be restarted with the proper timing."

Since at least one of the Peruvians worked in the healthcare field, I made a joke about the lack of informed-consent waivers.

But apparently we *did* have consent. "This morning we explained everything to *tu maestro,* and he gave consent."

This puzzled me but I moved on, asking Enrique how he had been able to defibrillate me. As a child, he explained, he had been set apart to live with the *altomisayoq* (high medicine elders). At the age of five, he was struck by lightning to begin his training. At twelve, he was struck again, and from that point on was recognized as being a "lightning-struck healer."

I thought for a moment and then said aloud, "We say that venom is like fire or lightning. We have a snake, the diamondback rattlesnake, that has what looks like two braided lightning bolts on its back." I pointed to my hatband, which had been made from just such an old friend. "It brings life or death. To be bitten by this snake is often called being 'struck by lightning.' Some medicine people will undergo it on purpose to gain the power it proffers."

Agitated conversation ensued. "You have done this, Brian?" I was asked.

"No, but I knew somebody who did, several times."

"*Yes!*" Enrique exclaimed. "*Tu maestro!* He stands beside you now, can you not see him?"

I had to admit I couldn't. But I asked Enrique, "If you see him, what color are his eyes?"

"Blue, like yours," he replied. "He is a little shorter. But of mixed blood like you."

I had to burst out laughing. That sounded like RT all right. Had he set the whole event in motion from wherever he then resided?

The Peruvians had another question. "The venom of this snake, what color is it?"

I thought back to milking. "Yellow," I said, "like lightning."

"*Amarillo intenso!*" exclaimed Enrique with a wide grin, clearly vindicated.

In retrospect, RT contacting me out of the blue five years earlier when he had phoned me to ask what my questions were may have been part of something larger. His training had prepared me to follow proper protocol with the spirits and Elders, and I had been found worthy of being kept alive for further spiritual training in both South and North America.

I never made it to Nevada, but never mind. RT has opened many doors for me, all over the world, and for that I am most grateful.

PART 3

Thunder People

Prophecies are not written in stone; all prophecies are
subject to change, especially if people have a change of heart.

ROLLING THUNDER

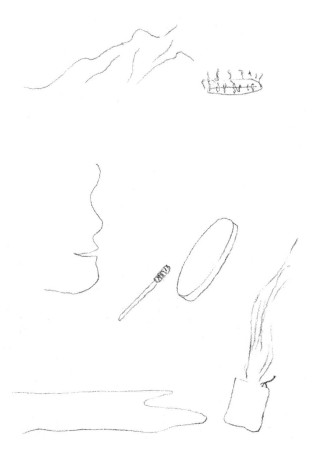

10
How Artwork Became Heart Work

Karie Garnier

KARIE GARNIER is a professional artist, an award-winning filmmaker, and a published author endorsed by UNESCO. As the visionary founder of Friends of Fuga he is leading a global campaign to save the ancient island of Fuga (in the northern Philippines) and protect it as a UNESCO World Heritage Site. He has enabled the giving of land titles to the Native Ilocano families who have lived on Fuga since ancient times and is helping them cocreate what he calls a healthy model village of the twenty-first century. Karie is the administrator of the Friends of Fuga community page on Facebook. To see the beauty of the ancient island, the documentary films, color photos, paintings, and the heart work inspired by Rolling Thunder, please visit www.facebook.com/SaveFugaIsland/. Karie's portrait of Rolling Thunder holding a golden eagle graced the cover of *The Voice of Rolling Thunder*. In this essay, he describes his profound healing and long friendship with RT, whom he believes helped him find the sacred island that called him to the South Seas to fulfill his life's purpose.

NO PHOTOS ALLOWED

The first time I met Rolling Thunder was on Saturday, August 14, 1982, on the outskirts of Falls City in the state of Washington. About fifty people from around the world had gathered to hear him speak about natural medicine and a few of us hoped to be healed. I was one of the sick people who needed healing.

During our two-day gathering, the traditional medicine man would not allow any of us to take his photograph. However, on the last day Rolling Thunder promised that we could take his picture after the morning session had ended. Finally, on Sunday at noon exactly, the healer announced that we could photograph him—but only for the next half hour. He warned us, "Any photos that you try to take of me after 12:30 will not turn out."

I got some good shots of Rolling Thunder before 12:30. Then, as he got up to walk away, I snapped a few more. I could hardly wait to see the results. When my photos of RT were developed, the shots that I captured before 12:30 proved to be good photos. However, in the last photos, (which I had snapped just after the 12:30 deadline), a dark gray cloud covered his face, making his features impossible to see.

THE NEAR-DEATH VISION

In the two years before I met Rolling Thunder, I had been deathly ill and clinging to life in White Rock, British Columbia. I suffered from multiple illnesses, including severe hypoglycemia, adrenal exhaustion, depression, and supraventricular tachycardia—my heart raced uncontrollably at two hundred beats a minute. On top of this I was skin and bones, my hair was falling out, I could barely speak, and I needed help to walk. My doctor warned me, "Your heart will not last much longer."

At the lowest point of my health crisis (January 1981) while I was facing death's door, I had a crazy dream. Some madman with a high-powered rifle was trying to shoot an eagle out of the sky. He aimed and fired off numerous rounds, but the great flying eagle dipped and dodged, flapped its big powerful wings, and transformed into a pair of high-powered galloping horses. With horrendous energy, the pair of charging horses thundered down from the heavens. They flew like two jets coming in for a landing, tearing across the plane of Earth and disappearing into the horizon.

Wow! What a dream! I woke up feeling dazed and confused.

My landlord was from Switzerland and happened to be a Jungian psychologist. He admonished me, "Karie, that's not a crazy dream! That's an archetypal dream and it's powerful. Your vision flew into you directly from God. It's trying to lead you on a journey. Pay attention and follow your vision and it will reveal who you really are. It's all about your purpose and who you are destined to become."

Shortly thereafter, I met Steven, another White Rock resident who had heard about my archetypal dream. Steven urged me, "Take that dream to Rolling Thunder. I met the man and I can assure you he's no lightweight."

A series of coincidences then led me to the weekend gathering where Rolling Thunder healed me. Simply listening to RT's voice and being in his presence created changes in my body. By the end of those two days I was filled with a fine energy and felt incredibly light on my feet. RT also prescribed two herbal roots that I was to boil into a tea and drink in a special way, and he gave me sage advice on how to maximize the healing process that would change my life forever. Later, I visited RT at his home in Carlin, Nevada, and continued to learn from him.

OUR ELDERS SPEAK

Inspired by my total healing with Rolling Thunder, over the next few years I traveled to reserved lands throughout the Pacific Northwest. I took part in First Nations ceremonies, and recorded on film and in print the images as well as quotations of several of the indigenous elders who were present.

Thanks to the far-reaching power of Rolling Thunder's medicines, my heart's work, an exhibit titled *Our Elders Speak—A Photographic Tribute*, was showcased at Expo 86 in Vancouver, at the British Columbia Museum of Anthropology, and at forty other public venues across the continent. The United Nations Association of Canada then presented the heartwarming photo panels at their conferences in Beijing and Moscow. Our message to the world was: "Let's celebrate a year of the Elder."

Due to the great interest in indigenous wisdom that the photo shows generated, in September 1990, CBC National Radio host Vicki Gabereau invited me to tell my Rolling Thunder healing story to the nation. Right after the broadcast, Vicki's producer phoned me and said, "Karie, the phone lines were ringing in our CBC offices all across Canada! We have never received so many phone calls from any of Vicki's previous guests." Due to popular demand, the CBC rated my story "the best of Gabereau" and broadcast the one-hour interview four times.

Following the broadcasts, I received more than a thousand letters from listeners who loved the interview. Almost all of the letters included checks for my coffee-table book *Our Elders Speak—A Tribute to Native Elders*, which, at this point, wasn't yet in print.

Collectors who own this critically acclaimed book of portraits and time-honored wisdom have noticed that I dedicated the publication to the two benevolent Elders who gave me life: my mother, Ferne, who was a natural healer, and my farseeing friend Rolling Thunder, who took me under his wing when I needed help the most. RT deeply inspired my lifework with Native people, and his teachings continue to inspire countless others as far away as Fuga Island in the South China Sea.

INITIATION BY LIGHTNING

But that's not the end of the story. Let me describe the initiation. In the summer of 1983, RT and his spiritual warriors climbed into an old blue Lincoln and drove all the way from Carlin, Nevada, to my seaside town of White Rock, British Columbia, which is a thousand miles to the north. Before RT arrived he phoned me and remarked, "There'll be an electrical storm." This statement was out of context with the rest of our conversation. And there was no sign of thunderclouds, let alone a storm.

Rolling Thunder arrived with his entourage and we all spent a pleasant four days together. After they left, an unprecedented electrical storm took place, which was awesome. For three and a half hours, thunder boomed and rolled across the sky above the black clouds that hung low over the water. The *boom! boom! boom!* of thunder rolling across the sky went on and on. Flashing forks of lightning repeatedly struck Semiahmoo Bay, sending residents and vacationers running for safety. While they ran from the electrical storm, climbed into their cars, and drove away, I felt the exact opposite. Feeling empowered—and in awe—I ran out onto the long wooden pier and into the very center of all the electricity. I stood there in the midst of the magic and for two hours I inhaled the fresh, raw energy of the storm and, in so doing, happily absorbed Rolling Thunder's gift.

I can remember that each time a lightning bolt struck the water in front of me I felt an intense twitch in the center of my solar plexus. The electricity was palpable, transformative, exhilarating, and literally hair-raising. A brave friend came out onto the White Rock pier to join me for the light show and, leaning forward and looking at my head, said "Oh, my God, Karie! Your hair is standing on end!"

I will never forget the climax of Rolling Thunder's electrical storm. One massive dazzling bolt of electricity split off into four arcs and effectively blew the metal lids from four 25,000-volt transformers that surrounded my subdivision. Meanwhile, all the lights in White Rock went out and the whole town was plunged into darkness.

I later noticed that these four burned-out transformers sat at the tops of power lines. They were four blocks apart and formed a rectangle that surrounded my home and the residential area on Marine Drive that RT had just vacated. On that electrifying night I remembered the advice

RT had offered during his stay in White Rock. I put out numerous pots and pans, collected the ensuing downpour of Thunder Water, and drank two quarts of Rolling Thunder's "medicine." That vital energy stayed inside me for days.

The peaceful feelings that the storm water had instilled in me intensified my intuition and began calling me into the wilderness. I felt the urge to get far away from civilization and I kept thinking, *I want to surrender and dive into nature.*

MY VISION QUEST

I thus embarked on my first solitary immersion in nature, traditionally known as the vision quest. Over the course of a decade I completed six of these ancient rites of passage. On each of the quests I fasted for four days and nights and, as instructed by the Elders, I asked the Great Spirit to clear my mind and reveal my purpose here on Earth.

Curiously, the vision quests repeatedly called me to find and become one with an ancient culture in the South Seas. I was not given the name of the country, only that it was somewhere south of China. Back in those early years, RT was very much alive, and he guided me on this journey that my near-death vision had triggered. I am eternally grateful to this sage who helped me find the primordial isle with its clan of three thousand beautiful Native Ilocanos.

I hereby attest that my healing with RT and the vision quests blessed and empowered my photographic work with the Elders. Additionally, Rolling Thunder's medicine and the "initiation by Lightning" awakened me to hear and heed my calling to the little-known island of Fuga, which in Latin means "escape." During my long friendship with RT, I witnessed his uncanny ability to tame wild animals and to call down lightning, thunder, and rain when they were needed, and—thanks to his benevolent intentions—totally heal a person's body, mind, and soul.

I can also attest that Rolling Thunder was—and still is—an

instrument of the Great Spirit, a technician of the sacred, a great healer, and the best friend I have ever had. RT is the seer who inspired me to find Fuga, produce several documentary films and websites about the island, and launch the global campaign that will hopefully mobilize cultural laws that will protect the ancient island forever.

Rolling Thunder was my most trusted personal advisor for my project "Our Elders Speak," as well as for the Fuga endeavor. On two occasions (including once in his kitchen in Carlin), he confided to me quietly, "You're one of my Thunder People."

Before RT died he also said (in our last conversation): "Karie, do you remember how I told you that I prayed for you and your work with the people of Fuga? Well, when I say that I prayed for you, I mean I prayed for you to have good things happen. I wish you great success!"

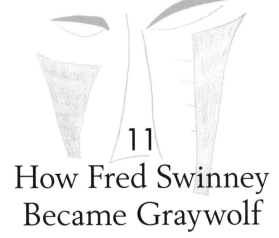

11

How Fred Swinney
Became Graywolf

Stanley Krippner, Ph.D.

STANLEY KRIPPNER, PH.D., is the Alan Watts Professor of Psychology at Saybrook University in Oakland, California, and past president of the Association for Humanistic Psychology and the International Association for the Study of Dreams. The recipient of several distinguished awards and the author and coauthor of many books, including *The Voice of Rolling Thunder* with Sidian Morning Star Jones, *Demystifying Shamans and Their World* with Adam Rock, *Personal Mythology,* and *Extraordinary Dreams and How to Work with Them,* he lives in San Rafael, California.

Fred Swinney had a successful counseling practice until the day in 1976 when his physician informed him that he would probably be dead within three years. He went on a camping trip to assimilate this shocking news and to take stock of his life. One night, in the Canadian wilderness, he fell asleep before his smoldering campfire and had a dream. In this dream, animal predators emerged from the woods and devoured

73

him. Awakening terrified, Swinney cast his eyes toward the coals of the fire. Just beyond the coals, he discerned two piercing eyes and the form of a large gray wolf. A feeling of total surrender replaced Swinney's fear, just as if he had become a wolf himself.

Upon returning to work, Swinney began to read about wolves and shamans. He discovered that his dream was a typical shamanic initiation dream, and that power animals were common allies of shamanic healers. Years later, writing for the *Dream Network Journal,* Swinney described what had happened to him on that fateful night:

> The eyes of the wolf brought me to this consciousness and held me there. There was a magnetic attraction; we communicated without word or sounds, open and vulnerable to each other. We seemed to exist in an endless moment beyond time and space. Eventually I noticed that the wolf shadow and eyes were gone but "wolfness" lingered in my mind. I was wolf! And then it was dawn and I knew I would survive. It was the essence of wolf that empowered and carried me through that time in the woods. I lived in a timeless state— foraging, intuitively finding roots, berries, and other plants to supplement the fish I caught. I returned to civilization four weeks later by the calendar, but an eternity later in subjective time (Swinney 1992, 18).

TAKING ON WOLF POWER

Gradually, Swinney introduced this "wolf consciousness" into his counseling practice. Oftentimes he had insights into his clients' conditions that defied any rational explanation. At one point, he thought he might have lycanthropy, a term psychiatrists use to describe a condition in which people believe themselves to *be* wolves. He knew that within Native American cultures this condition was not uncommon, but that knowledge did not diminish his fears. Nonetheless, he continued to practice psychotherapy and also kept reading about wolves, discovering aspects of himself that resonated with the behavior of these animals.

Swinney came to me and asked for advice. I helped him identify aspects of himself that had been suppressed all of his life, traits that matched what he had learned about wolves and their behavior. These shadowy aspects of Swinney's character came to the surface. Self-confidence and self-acceptance replaced fear and anxiety and, eventually, Fred Swinney was replaced by Graywolf.

In 1980, at a conference sponsored by the Association for Humanistic Psychology, Swinney told his story and formally took the name Graywolf. I was in the audience and observed the encouragement that the newly named Graywolf received. At this point, I suggested that Graywolf visit Rolling Thunder. The visit turned into a lengthy learning experience as Graywolf began to feel more and more comfortable participating in shamanic rituals and healing sessions. Eventually, Graywolf established the Asklepia Foundation, named after the Greek god of healing who reputedly came to people in their dreams, near Grants Pass, Oregon. At this retreat, Graywolf taught people how to heal themselves through dreams, diet, exercise, and ritual.

Graywolf outlived his physician's death warrant by three decades, using what he had learned from Rolling Thunder as well as what his own dreams and inner wolf had revealed to him.

12

Life Should Be
Beautiful for Everyone

Jean Millay, Ph.D.

JEAN MILLAY, PH.D., is a writer, graphic artist, prize-winning filmmaker, psychical researcher, and pioneer in the use of biofeedback in education. Her doctoral dissertation centered on a pioneering experiment in which telepathy was attempted between pairs of intimate friends whose brain waves were being monitored. She is the author of *Multidimensional Mind* and the editor/author of *Silver Threads: 25 Years of Parapsychology Research* and *Radiant Minds: Scientists Explore the Dimensions of Consciousness*. In 1972, Rolling Thunder participated in the Association for Humanistic Psychology's first conference focused on a particular topic, in this case, self-healing. It was held in San Francisco, where Jean Millay obtained permission to interview him. The following text highlights some of the wisdom that RT shared, in his own words, during this interview.

The first rule of Native American healing is compassion. If people don't have compassion and concern, they will never become any type of spiritual person or healer. But there is a wide gap between *spiritual* and *religious*. *Religious* comes from the word *religio*, which means "to regiment." I think people are getting far too civilized and regimented. Now some people want to be spiritual and they think that the only way to be spiritual is to learn more big words, words that they can hide behind, and to invent new religions based on them. Many are experimenting with drugs, meditation, and different things wherein they lose sight of the basis of any religion and our purpose in being, which is to have real concern for our fellow humans.

The basic teaching of the Native American spiritual way of life is that the object of being here is to do something each day of our lives to make life better for others. I would like to see more people stop being religious and start being spiritual—to do something, or to speak out, or to do whatever they can do.

I think that people should learn to think with a clear mind. They should first work on clearing their minds by good thinking, speaking good things, praying, and fasting. The minds of too many people have become clouded. All this pollution comes from the minds of modern people. Their brains are cluttered up with trash—or, worse, with aggression, greed, and fear. The human brain is so big and has so much capacity, but if it's cluttered up with trash and limited in narrow ways of thinking, it can't have room to create the good things.

The ancient people who built the pyramids and started the great civilizations had clear minds. They knew how to use the energy of the natural forces so that it was unlimited. They could think in many different ways and had powerful ways of focusing energy, even in healing broken bones or broken spirits. They could create whatever they needed for transportation and other things, without causing pollution.

At one time people around the world had the same beliefs. They knew the same laws about Mother Earth and the Father Sun and the Creator. But civilized humans have gotten away from this. They are too regimented, too greedy, and too warlike. The only way to bring peace and harmony is when people have more understanding of each other, of animals, of nature, of themselves, and their own families. And then we can begin to understand how justice can be brought about and how people can get along with each other. This is the real healing process.

People have to change their thinking, not according to some religious concept, but according to the Great Spirit's way of living and thinking in harmony with nature. Life should be beautiful for everyone. Some think this is radical thinking. We call it spiritual thinking.

13
Walking with the Truth

Kenneth Cohen

KENNETH COHEN is a renowned health and cultural educator who operates at the forefront of the dialogue between ancient wisdom and contemporary science. A qigong master (qigong is a form of Chinese healing exercise) as well as a traditional healer who has been mentored since his youth by indigenous elders, he is the author of *Honoring the Medicine: The Essential Guide to Native American Healing* and *The Way of Qigong*. On a visit to the Rocky Mountains, he and Rolling Thunder spoke about what their perspectives had in common. Portions of this dialogue were published in *Voice of Thunder*, the Meta Tantay newsletter.

ROLLING THUNDER: Ho! *Osiyo* ["Hello" in Cherokee]. We are sitting up here in a place called Boulder Canyon in the Rocky Mountains. In our conversations we have found no differences between the teachings of ancient spiritual ways of life, or religions as some people call them. We are going to talk about these teachings. Some of this knowledge was nearly lost, and yet if it were applied today there would be less pollution, less sickness, less of all that's bad.

People today are looking for better ways of doing things. They're also looking for consolation. So many people in this civilized society are wound up like a spring. The chiropractors are doing wonderful business. My doctor friends give the same reports. We are going to put it out in such a way that maybe they'll do less. We say that anything that helps is good. We're not fanatical. But moderation in all things is one of the Indian laws.

KENNETH COHEN: Ho! The Chinese term for religion is *Tsung Chiao;* this means "ancestral or original teachings." And in China this is best represented by Taoism. The word *Tao* itself means "the way," in the sense of "the way of nature," which is the natural way for people to live.

The Taoist tradition has two roots. One of these roots is the indigenous people of China, including what the anthropologists like to call the shamans, who at one time were spread throughout China. A lot of these tribal people are still out there in western China, and they are facing some of the same challenges that Native American people have faced here.

The other root was the philosopher-recluses who withdrew from China's complex and war-torn society around the fourth century BCE. They went off into the mountains to learn the ways of nature and escape the chaos that was occurring during this time in China's history. This combination [shamanism and spiritual practices of the recluses] joined together to establish the Taoist spiritual way or Taoist tradition. Over a period of centuries, various styles or schools of Taoism developed, with each sect emphasizing something a little bit different. As in Native American culture, diversity is the rule.

One of these is *Tao Shih,* which denotes a person who has studied the spiritual teachings and received initiations. However, unlike similar customs in Native American traditions, this individual is also ordained. The word *shih* means "a person who is devoted to learning," thus the term.

The next-higher stage is called the *Tao Jen*, which designates a person who is really living the spiritual way of life. She is not only studying, but is living it, "walking the talk," which is considerably more important.

Next is the level known as *Chen Jen. Chen* means "truth." *Jen* means "person." So *Chen Jen* means "person of truth." My Taoist teacher defined it this way: "*Chen Jen* is the person whose inside matches his or her outside." In other words, there is no hypocrisy; one is always directly seeking the truth.

Finally, the highest stage of all in the Taoist tradition is simply the person who is living in harmony with nature, which is known as the *Hsien Jen*. The Chinese character for this is a picture of a man or woman living in the mountains.

ROLLING THUNDER: The similarities in the teachings from China, the Taoists, and our own American Indian traditions are amazing. Thunder People are people of truth. And it is the same over in Scandinavia and Greece—everywhere around the world. In the old days it was known that the Thunder God meant truth. Rolling Thunder means "song to the gods" or "walking with the truth," and truth is what we are looking for. We are looking for Thunder People now and we need them.

This conversation took place in 1982, at my home, a log cabin that is located nine thousand feet high in the Rocky Mountains, at the border of Colorado's Indian Peaks Wilderness. I believe it was to protect my privacy that Rolling Thunder kindly mentioned only the nearby "Boulder Canyon," rather than revealing the name of the specific area where I lived. At that time I was midway through a formal apprenticeship with Rolling Thunder, learning songs, ceremonial ways, healing methods, and, most important, culture and values. I was spending a few months a year living at Meta Tantay, where I continued my training and also taught basic qigong to contribute to the health of the community.

There was no money exchanged, given that Rolling Thunder was adamant that spirituality was a gift, and neither ceremony nor healing should ever have a price.

I was deeply honored when Rolling Thunder and several of his "warriors" (students and community members) visited me in Colorado. In accord with traditional protocol, he reached out to a local Denver-based Elder Wallace Black Elk (Lakota) to invite him to be the first speaker at a public lecture at Boulder High School, in Boulder, Colorado. I was the second speaker. Before his own presentation, Rolling Thunder introduced us and then, as always, spoke about the differences between indigenous values and those of mainstream Euro-American society, as well as the continuing abuses and injustices faced by Native Americans. Small-minded individuals who over the years accused him of commercializing or giving away secrets never met Rolling Thunder. He saw value in his celebrity only because it allowed more people to become aware of Native issues. With his passing, the Indian world lost not only a great medicine man but also one of its strongest activists and warriors.

14
Mother Earth Is Our
Great Mentor

Carolyna Saint Germain

CAROLYNA SAINT GERMAIN is the author of *Stewards for the Earth*. In addition to being a midwife, she officiates and teaches ceremonies that she calls Blessingways. These practices allow one to experience mindful awareness and conscious connection to our Mother Earth. Here are her recollections of Rolling Thunder.

My husband, Norman Cohen, and I will always remember two of our favorite, respected, and beloved people, Rolling Thunder (John Pope) and his loving and kindhearted wife Spotted Fawn. Although they have both crossed over to another place, they remain very dear to our hearts and we speak of them often with great fondness.

We had the privilege of meeting Rolling Thunder and Spotted Fawn in Los Angeles after we had read the book by Doug Boyd titled *Rolling Thunder*. Little did we know that when we set out for the evening engagement at which we would meet them, our longtime quest for spiritual understanding and transformation would finally begin to accelerate. My husband and I were curious and intrigued with the mysteries of the natural world and had both been reading transpersonal and metaphysical philosophies, which kept us up into the wee hours of the morning. We were seeking a spiritual direction that would resonate with our natural being, one that we could incorporate into our daily lives, unfolding from within. Rolling Thunder entered our lives at this moment in time, proving indeed the truth of the old adage "When the student is ready, the master appears."

The continuing revolutionary spirit of the 1960s and early 1970s was deeply embedded in us. As "revolutionary activists" we felt that the sociopolitical consciousness had to shift and change. Our first exchange with Rolling Thunder was about ideas of change. We came to understand that change can only come from within, and that this process benefitted and was enhanced by living in small communities in natural settings. This combination allows for the opportunity to fully and, with an open heart, experience oneself and others. This is what Earth, our Great Mother, teaches and personifies in all her aspects. As I wrote in my book *Stewards for the Earth,*

> The oak grows next to the evergreen, the river runs into the sea, the wind and the rain are granted free rein. The Earth's natural possessions are resourced and consumed unrelentingly, without ever a grumble, nor an inkling of resentful bitterness. She is the ultimate, unsurpassed, unconditional Giver. In every aspect she exhibits compassionate coexistence and undeniable bounty. She displays exceptional qualities: unprecedented generosity, all-inclusive diversity, magnanimous acceptance and allowance, quiet wisdom and infinitely wide ranging magnificent beauty. She is clothed in vibrant colors, dramatic landscapes, and liquid light and shadow; offering all the possible hues, shades, textures, aromas, resonances, palettes, and perceptions. These are benevolent gifts, bestowed upon all of us who live here, without exception.

WHAT ROLLING THUNDER TAUGHT US

The Mother Earth is our great mentor. Through her unceasing and perpetual example, she demonstrates allowance and acceptance of all things. Emulating her is truly possible. Rolling Thunder and Spotted Fawn quietly personified this teaching in their daily lives and we were eager to learn from them.

Rolling Thunder told us from the very beginning, "Watch your thoughts. Whatever you think, you become and create in your lives." Even though this is a common saying today, at that time it was a less widely known and accepted concept. It is true also that every spiritual teacher has expounded on this principle, but we had the privilege of observing Rolling Thunder *living* that truth. Through the experience of his example, he taught us how to live with an awareness of our thoughts.

We recall the sunrise ceremony held at the beginning of the day. During this ceremony, our thoughts, prayers, and intentions were instilled into a little mound of tobacco resting in the palm of our hands. It was then offered to the four directions: the North, South, East, and West; to the elements of Fire, Air, Earth, and Water; to the Father Sun, Mother Earth, and Grandmother Moon. These thoughts create our day. This is a simple, extremely powerful ceremony. The smoke from the fire, the drumming, and the welcome song all conspired together to send our prayers to the Great Spirit. The energy of the circle spiraled out and up to the Great Beyond, to the land of Spirit.

Rolling Thunder taught us all this.

Rolling Thunder was not afraid to tell the long-haired white folks how to live in harmony with the Mother Earth and be connected with the Great Spirit. He held no prejudice against us, the descendants of the white persecutors. He told us that the prophecies spoke of the time when the white man and woman would become interested in the Native American and the tribal-clan spiritual way of life. And it was then that the Mother Earth would begin to make her changes.

He hoped to see it, and I guess he did. Things don't always appear as they seem. Only the Great Spirit knows the right time and place for everything. We can only continue to pray for "what is good and meant to be, and to all of our relations" and offer our tobacco to the morning fire.

THE FIRST VISIT TO NEVADA

The first time I went to Carlin was life altering on many levels. For the first twelve hours I was there, I went from involuntarily holding my breath to gasping for air. I realized later that I could not have prepared myself for the emotional roller-coaster ride I would experience here in Carlin. Rolling Thunder owned a few lots at the end of a little street in this very small, high-desert Nevada town. The locals already spoke of him as "this crazy Injun," but as he became more renowned because of the aforementioned book and the lectures he was giving all over the country and world, he began to receive many guests. Then the locals began to worry that he would take over the place! In his amicable way Rolling Thunder received everyone with equal respect and honor and created all the necessary accommodations to feed and house his guests and patients. There were wickiups (traditional Native American huts made with willows and covered with hides) and small travel trailers all over his property.

There were also lots and lots of people of all ages. Some were busy with the task of feeding the crowd and others with making up beds for the new arrivals. There were children running underfoot and in and out of the woodshed and work sheds and harassing the chickens, ducks, and geese. It was truly a melee!

Inside the little box house where Rolling Thunder and Spotted Fawn lived was a very small kitchen crammed with women cooking the evening meal for all these people. And, oh yes, one very small bathroom! Coming from Beverly Hills, California, Norman and I could not have imagined this scene if we'd tried. But we loved it!

We loved Spotted Fawn at first sight. She was the matriarch and clan mother to this eclectic crowd of Native Americans, African Americans, Mexicans, Puerto Ricans, Asians, and whites. She emanated pure unconditional love. That doesn't mean she was a pushover! She had rules and regulations and one had better follow them or there would be hell to pay. And hell existed right here on Mother Earth. But she was so loving, sincere, and wonderful that no one ever wanted to cross her, except maybe her own children. (It seems as if we always have to test our parents!)

Norman went to sit with the men in the arbor outside, where Rolling Thunder was giving a lecture, teaching some young people from Europe about the correct way to pick herbs and take the bounty from Mother Earth. You never just take something from the Mother Earth without asking if it is permitted by the plant or tree, and making a prayer of thanksgiving. Then you give something in return: some tobacco, a coin, or some of your hair.

I slipped away from this group and went to the little kitchen to offer my help to the women. I started helping to cook, clean, wash dishes, and perform other kinds of womanly chores. I was involved in the women's consciousness-raising movement at that time, and I should have been bothered by these seemingly distinct male-female roles, but somehow it just seemed like such a natural part of what was going on in Carlin. I instinctively understood the authentic mutual respect among the sexes, despite the age differences and cultural diversities.

Rolling Thunder was very willing to explain his ideas and understanding of the male-female balance at the dinner table that night. As he did so, I remember thinking that he was reading my mind! Twelve men and boys all crowded around the big kitchen table on one side of the room. They ate first and were served by the women. I figured the men ate first because there was not much room for everyone to sit. This was true, but the real reason for the separation of the men and women was to allow for bonding to take place. I enjoyed sitting with the women and girls afterward. And it was a good bonding time.

That first night, after all the cleanup was done, we were about twenty people crowded in the front room on two old sofas and chairs or sitting on the floor. I became sort of mesmerized listening to Rolling

Thunder as he smoked his corncob pipe. He spoke about the condition of the Native American people in America. He shared that the white people wanted all the Indians to become assimilated into their culture and throw away their own culture and beliefs. He told us the story of the Trail of Tears, when the Cherokee were moved from east of the Mississippi to Oklahoma, twelve hundred miles away. More than five thousand Cherokee—men, women, and children—died on the Trail of Tears due to starvation and the white man's diseases of smallpox, measles, cholera, malaria, and whooping cough. These Indians were not allowed to perform the sacred ceremonies for their dead. They were humiliated, forced to move from their homes, and almost annihilated.

Rolling Thunder took on the anguish and torment of this march. His voice rose and fell over us in waves of sorrow, regret, compassion, and forgiveness. It became a trail of tears for me too. I couldn't stop weeping; neither could I hide my distress and tears. He looked over at me, his dark eyes shooting lightning bolts. He knew that he had found a compatriot and friend. I never said a word to him personally during our whole three-day visit but we were definitely psychically and spiritually connected. Norman had the honor and opportunity of being at his side the whole time and he shared Rolling Thunder's wisdom with me on the long drive home.

ROLLING THUNDER'S PRAGMATIC
WISDOM TO LIVE BY

Rolling Thunder's pragmatic and tribal wisdom to live by can be summarized in some general statements:

- The clan mother is the only one who can dehorn a chief; all she has to do is pack his things and put his bag outside their tipi.
- There is no need for lawyers when a couple is divorced; all you have to do is just change your tipi.
- Walk your talk or be quiet.

- Respect one another.
- Respect yourself.
- Never touch anyone else's belongings without asking.
- At meetings, if no conclusion can be reached, the women will call for a food break, and when the meeting is resumed, a consensus is achieved because everyone has had time to think.
- It is necessary to listen to the opinions of women and gain from the woman's intuition and wisdom without losing face.
- When a warrior goes to war with another tribe, if a killing occurs, the warrior is not allowed back into the camp until he purifies himself through fasting, prayer, and solitude, in order to make amends with the dead. (This teaching was especially appropriate in relation to the mass murders happening during the Vietnam War. But in all wars, glorified killing should never be the standard.)
- The positions in the tribe are all equal, it is a circle.
- Shamans are born gifted, but they have to pass the Great Spirit's tests in order to be humble enough to be healers.
- Chiefs are appointed by the circle for their strength, courage, intelligence, compassion, leadership, and commitment to the circle.
- Always make an offering to the Mother Earth and Spirit when taking something from the earth such as plants, feathers, and rocks.
- Show love and respect for the Mother Earth, above all else. It is our home.
- We are *all* connected.

REMINISCING ABOUT ROLLING THUNDER

Norman and I and some of our friends brought Rolling Thunder a big movie-lot truck that became known as the Billy Jack truck. It had been used during the making of the *Billy Jack* movie, which was loosely based on part of the life of Rolling Thunder and in which Rolling Thunder played a small role. We heavily loaded it down with everything we could jam into it: boxes of nails, carpets, tools, foodstuffs, furniture, a huge variety of clothing, and donations from our friends and associates in the Topanga Canyon, Beverly Hills, and greater Los Angeles area.

This "mobile masterpiece" was driven to Carlin and unloaded by Rolling Thunder's sons and warriors, who included Buffalo Horse, Spotted Eagle, Running Bear, and all the other "boys" in the group. Norman (our Jewish prince!) was present and was thrown a fifty-pound box of nails. He staggered under the weight of it and almost dropped it, but "held on for dear life!" he would later exclaim while retelling the story. Of course, all the warriors smirked and hid behind their politeness, but as Norman would go on to explain,

> when the weight of the carpets that we tossed from the truck brought me to my knees I saw Rolling Thunder chewing really hard on his pipe to keep from laughing, too. I wondered what these guys were doing to me. However, I kept my own sense of humor and told a joke (I was famous for having the right joke at the right time!) and then everybody could laugh and feel comic relief, including me. Later Rolling Thunder told me that if the men didn't respect or like me they wouldn't bother to tease me and mess with me. It was a way of expressing affection. I could relate to that. We all became close friends and brothers over the many years.

Norman also remembers these funny stories:

> I went out to the land one time with Buffalo Horse and Carolyna, before it became Meta Tantay and it was occupied by the Rolling Thunder tribe of Thunder People. There was only Greg, the Puerto Rican, out there serving as the caretaker. We were going to smoke a pipe or two and enjoy the night sky. Well, we got to the gate and since I was riding shotgun, I jumped out to unlock and open the gate. Everything went fine. However, on the way out, I jumped out and

opened the gate, Buffalo Horse drove through, and then I closed and locked the gate with me on the wrong side. I had locked myself in! Well, we all laughed ourselves into tears over that! It was another classic Norman maneuver.

On another occasion, Buffalo Horse and I were sent to get a load of gravel. RT was having a gathering at the house and he wanted to put gravel on all the pathways so folks wouldn't have to walk in the mud. We drove around, I thought to the gravel yard, or somewhere where he had already made arrangements to pick the gravel up. We got there and started loading the bed of the old Dodge station wagon. Well, I never saw someone shovel so fast in my life. Buffalo Horse shoveled three or four shovelfuls to my one. He was amazing! He got tired of my bragging about him, the greatest shoveler ever. I told that story a hundred times!

One day, many years later, he told me, "The truth is, Norman, that gravel wasn't ours!" No wonder he shoveled so fast. Go figure!

One time we were all with RT, having a fabulous Italian dinner, made by a friend of mine. There were about twelve men sitting around the table. It was a great feast and celebration. At the end of the meal, a pipe was brought out and RT loaded it with his famous Five Brothers tobacco. Well, I was overwhelmed to be smoking with everyone in this ceremony of brotherhood. So, when my turn came, I took a hit of this twenty-five-cents-a-package tobacco, inhaling deep into my lungs, and I turned red, then green. I didn't want to have a coughing fit but, man, I was dying. My eyes were watering, I was sweating and finally I had to cough, choking nearly to death! Rolling Thunder says I disappeared, probably under the table. Maybe I did. I sure felt like disappearing!

Several years later, Carolyna and I owned the Thunder Trading Company and Frontier Deli in Santa Cruz, California. Rolling

Thunder would come and spent lots of time with us there as it was a great center of operation for his talks all around the San Francisco Bay area and farther south. We so much enjoyed and appreciated his visits. With his entourage of singers and drummers and security team, he would go out into the garden of our restaurant and drum and sing. Everyone from all around would come and be uplifted by the singing and drumming. He helped us create a great business.

One day Rolling Thunder, along with one of his dear friends, Grandfather Semu, and I were sitting in the sun at a garden table eating our wonderful food. They started talking about giving me an Indian name. Well, I had always wanted an Indian name but god forbid that I would ever say anything like that. I was very aware how Rolling Thunder felt about Indians giving white people Indian names. This was something that generally did not sit very well with him.

Despite this, I got very excited but tried hard not to show it. Then Rolling Thunder began to speak about the eagle, what it meant symbolically, its significance, and its nature. He looked up at the blue sky and I followed his gaze, expecting a giant eagle to show up right then and there. He looked down and became quiet, chewing on his pipe. So Grandfather Semu took up the narrative. He spoke about the hawk, expounding on its significance. Then they both sat very still and were quiet for quite a while.

I stayed as calm as possible but I certainly was fidgety.

At last Rolling Thunder looked up at me with his black-as-night eyes and spoke again. Without one bit of humor, nor a twinkle in his eye, he quietly said, "We have decided that your name will be Bagel Feather." Total silence. I wasn't sure whether I should laugh or not, or if it was a joke or what. Then, in all earnestness Rolling Thunder told me that we should always honor and be proud of where we come from. Since I was a Jewish Indian, part of the lost tribe, then I should always be proud of that.

I tell everyone that story now, and people always laugh, but for me it has great meaning and sincerity. It took me a few years to

understand the significance and the wisdom of my name and I honor
the great man who saw me for who I am and I profoundly respect the
name Bagel Feather.

Rolling Thunder conducted numerous healing ceremonies in our presence. It is difficult to recount all of those events because they were all "otherworldly": the intensity of the drumming and singing, the burning of the cedar, his actions as a medicine man, the energy in the room. These were times of powerful witnessing to the work of Spirit moving and coming through the open vessel that was Rolling Thunder. They were transcendental and transpersonal experiences. We never talked about them much. They were sacred. Rolling Thunder did heal people. I saw it, and I witnessed the transformation that occurred during these events, not only on the patient, but on everyone involved—even those in the household.

Some of these healings happened in our California homes in Topanga Canyon and Santa Cruz. Our living quarters were blessed as a result. Rolling Thunder named our two sons at the time of their births by interpreting the dreams of all those who were present at the time. These names are sacred to us and our sons, Big Man and Sunrise Strong Heart. There are many other RT stories that I could share, but the ones included here will serve to tell the people who read them how Rolling Thunder and Spotted Fawn changed the direction of our lives.

Rolling Thunder is our relation in the world of Spirit now. We have a benefactor in the Great Beyond. He is with us in our daily lives too, because he lives and breathes in the hearts of all his Thunder People, and my husband, Bagel Feather, and I are very proud to number among them.

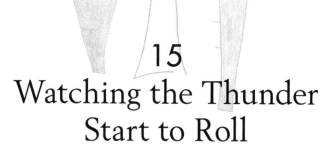

15
Watching the Thunder
Start to Roll

Kanya Vashon McGhee

KANYA VASHON MCGHEE founded the Tree of Life Book Store in Harlem, New York, in 1969. As a result of political maneuvering, it was torn down in 1980 and replaced by a parking lot, but during its peak years it attracted some fifteen thousand people per month who enjoyed its many books that covered a wide range of spiritual, historical, and psychological topics. At our request, Kanya reminisced about his meeting with RT.

In the late 1970s, I was driving cross-country from New York to California. Someone had suggested that I look up Rolling Thunder, because we had many shared interests. I located his home in Carlin, Nevada, and was lucky he was there. We took an immediate liking to each other. It was like we were family members. Perhaps it was because we shared blood in common through the Cherokees. My paternal grandmother, Maidee Moselle Haywood McGhee, was a full-blooded Cherokee, and RT was part Cherokee. He was also a decade my senior and seemed like my uncle or elder brother.

RT told me about the intertribal/interracial community he had formed, called Meta Tantay, a Chumash term meaning "go in peace." This community taught people to work cooperatively following the principles found in Native American wisdom traditions. The residences were wickiups—domes built out of willows and covered with rugs, which were, according to RT, warm in the winter and cool in the summer. But the Meta Tantay wickiups were unique because of their composition. In 1972, the well-known environmental artist Christo had built what he dubbed the Running Fence. This construction was made from white Mylar plastic erected through parts of California's Sonoma and Marin counties. The project took forty-two months, and over the course of that time entailed eighteen public hearings and three court sessions to see it through. When the project's lease expired in 1976, Christo donated the material to Meta Tantay and a few other projects that he liked. As a result, the wickiups were constructed from Christo's Mylar.

INJUSTICE AT THE HANDS OF THE WHITES

We stopped at a tourist center and the officer in charge started his spiel about the white settlers and the Indians working harmoniously together. That is when I observed the "thunder" start to roll. RT was furious about having to listen to what he considered a glossing over of history and the injustice done to Native Americans by white settlers. RT pointed out that millions of Native Americans died as a result of the European invasion, most of them from disease brought by the settlers. The assaults on their lands, their cultures, and their religions have left a devastating legacy that is still in need of healing.

I resonated with what RT said because it reminded me of the way politicians had attained control of the Harlem property on which my bookstore, the Tree of Life, was located. The convention hotel for which the land was needed never materialized, and now a parking lot sits on the site. Fortunately, I was able to take the Tree of Life to the Internet to continue the sale of unique and unusual books there.

I was with RT for only a few hours, but I will never forget the experience and what he taught me. He made a very deep impression on me because of his integrity and spiritual largesse.

FOUR ASCENTS OF THE HOOP AND A VISION UNFULFILLED

RT is often included on lists of Native American prophets, joining such luminaries as Black Elk, Wovoka, Thomas Banyaca, Lame Deer, and Sun Bear. Contrary to Western views of time—with a past, a present, and a future—Native American traditions view time as a cycle or a hoop, each turn or ascent of the hoop being a preparation for the next.

In 1872, Black Elk was nine years of age. He had a vision of four ascents of the hoop, of the four generations that he would know. At the first ascent, Black Elk saw people camped around a sacred tree. At the second ascent, leaves began to fall from the tree, indicating that a way of life was coming to an end. At the third turn, at the same camp, he saw the holy tree dying, all its birds having flown away. That was the time of the generation living in the 1850s, their hoop broken. Black Elk saw himself standing on top of a mountain where he could see that the hoop of his people was one of several hoops. In the middle was a revivified world tree that sheltered all the children on Earth. Black Elk never saw the promise of the fourth aspect come into being. He died in 1950, feeling that his people's hoop was still broken.

Near the end of the nineteenth century, Indians were being forced onto reservations. Buffalo had been slaughtered to near extinction and various traditions, such as the ghost dance, had been banned. A Native American prophet by the name of Jack Wilson took the name of Wovoka, "the One Who Makes Live," and renewed the hope of his people. The Oglala Sioux tribe sent three of its leaders to meet with

Wovoka; the group brought back positive reports. Like Black Elk, Wovoka had a positive vision about the future, one in which another world was coming, one that would arrive like a cloud, bringing fresh buffalo with it. But this vision was derailed in 1890 at Wounded Knee, South Dakota, where nearly three hundred Indians who were on their way to a ghost dance were killed by U.S. troops.

Like other Native American traditions, these prophecies are rooted in myth, magic, and metaphor. And it must be remembered that when the prophecies speak of death and dying, they could be referring to the death of dysfunctional ways of thinking and behaving. When the prophecies speak of new worlds arising, they may be speaking of new ways of viewing Earth and humanity's place on it. This is the hopeful, benevolent view.

In 1976, Thomas Banyaca, a Hopi Indian Elder, addressed a conference sponsored by the United Nations in Vancouver, Canada. He called upon the United Nations to avert the disaster foretold by Hopi prophecies, disasters brought about by oppression of traditional people and by the destruction of the natural environment. Although these disasters are impending, they can be averted if people return to some semblance of a reasonable balance with the environment, which was upset when they started to exploit Earth rather than living harmoniously with it.

This prediction of disaster was one that Rolling Thunder made repeatedly. For him, ecological imbalance was like a cancer that can spread over the body if it is not arrested in time. For RT, Earth was a living organism, an organism that wanted to be well, and would take drastic measures to retain its health if the threat continued. RT often observed that when people harm the Earth, they harm themselves, and when they harm themselves, they harm the Earth.

Lame Deer and Sun Bear, two twentieth-century Native American prophets, underscored the same theme. Lame Deer claimed that people were becoming too reliant on machines and electric power. This dependency made people weak, vulnerable, and an "endangered species." Sun Bear shared this bleak vision of people who were so alienated from their environment that they would have no way to support themselves in times of crisis. When electricity runs out or the grid is down, when water runs dry, and when oil is depleted, people will abandon the huge cities and this will force them to return to the land and seek advice from its earlier, Earth-honoring custodians, the Native Americans.

16
When Nixon Did the
Right Thing

Stanley Krippner, Ph.D.

STANLEY KRIPPNER, PH.D., is the Alan Watts Professor of Psychology at Saybrook University in Oakland, California, and past president of the Association for Humanistic Psychology and the International Association for the Study of Dreams. The recipient of several distinguished awards and the author and coauthor of many books, including *The Voice of Rolling Thunder* with Sidian Morning Star Jones, *Demystifying Shamans and Their World* with Adam Rock, *Personal Mythology*, and *Extraordinary Dreams and How to Work with Them*, he lives in San Rafael, California.

When I first heard RT give lectures, he would invariably rant and rave about the Indian children who had been kidnapped and put into Euro-American homes. At first I thought this claim was hyperbole. But after doing some research, I discovered that RT was absolutely on target.

This all started with the official governmental policy of assimilation. Indians were regarded as incompetent parents and many children were indeed "kidnapped" and placed for adoption or were given outright to white parents. Many other children were sent to boarding schools that were sponsored by the Bureau of Indian Affairs. At these schools they were told to stop using their native language and were forbidden to engage in tribal practices. The Bureau of Indian Affairs formed the Indian Adoption Project, which lasted from 1958 to 1967, yet as late as 1971 about 17 percent of young Indians were removed from their families. A decade earlier, the figure had been 30 percent. These were the years when RT was making his outrageous claims, but they were not exaggerations.

The philosophy behind assimilation was "kill the Indian and save the man." In other words, Indian survival was contingent on assimilating them into mainstream American culture. Moreover, many Native American women were sterilized so that the Indian population could be further reduced (Corntassel and Witmer 2008). Rolling Thunder also brought forced sterilization to his audience's attention. This may have been one of many reasons why someone shot a bullet into his house while he was relaxing on the sofa. Fortunately, the attempted assassin was a bad shot, but I saw the bullet hole in the wall, as did many of RT's other guests over the years.

Forced assimilation simply didn't work. Instead, Native Americans began asking for self-determination, a reversal of the paternalistic policies that had been forced upon them, resulting in the abolition of many Native-governing types of councils. Self-determination was the means by which a tribe reconstituted itself by implementing its own sovereign powers and policies. One example was the establishment of Native American colleges and universities where cultural traditions could be preserved and taught.

THE FIGHT FOR SELF-DETERMINATION

The Indian Reorganization Act of 1934 initiated self-determination, although many politicians and lobbyists prevented its full implementation. In addition, the goal of the act still focused on making Indians proper American citizens. During the 1950s, politicians and lobbyists tried to erase these modest gains, recommending termination of tribal governments. Again, the goal was assimilation and about one hundred tribes were taken off of the official records.

In 1970, there was a major breakthrough when President Richard Nixon addressed the issue in his congressional message, Recommendations for Indian Policy. Nixon proclaimed, "The time has come to break decisively with the past and to create the condition for a new era in which the Indian future is determined by Indian acts and Indian decisions." This proclamation formally terminated the assimilation policy because it was followed by the implementation of the 1968 Indian Civil Rights Act, the initiation in 1974 of the Indian Financing Act, the 1975 Self-Determination and Education Act, the 1978 Religious Freedom Act, and, during the same year, the Indian Child Welfare Act. The latter act recognized tribal courts as the primary forum for the welfare and custody cases concerning Indian children (Wilkins 2010).

In commenting on Nixon's support for tribal courts, the author Louise Erdrich told a *TIME* magazine reporter (Luscombe 2015) that previous treaties held that tribal courts could not prosecute a non-Native who committed a crime in Indian country. "The first person who tried to fix this was Richard Nixon, who read the treaties and, as a true conservative, realized that certain rights should be inherent." During Nixon's years in office, the sacred Blue Lake was returned to the people of the Taos Pueblo (1970), a special office on Indian water rights was established (1973), and the Menominee tribe was reconstituted (1973). Nixon did not act unilaterally. Indian activists played a major role in making these changes. In 1972, some of them occupied the offices of the Bureau of Indian Affairs for a week, and the same year Native American militants confronted federal forces in Wounded Knee, South Dakota, for seventy-two days. The American Indian Movement was a potent force, and Rolling Thunder attended many of their confrontations, even visiting Alcatraz Island when AIM occupied it for several months between 1969 and 1971. A few U.S. senators such as Edward Kennedy and Henry Jackson helped get the legislation through Congress. And many organizations, some of which I am a member, attempted to mobilize grassroots support.

Despite his many failings, Nixon was one of the most dynamic supporters of Indian rights to occupy the White House. Why? In a revealing statement, Nixon commented that he had always admired his Native American college football coach because the coach taught him the principles of fair play. Because he resigned the presidency in disgrace in 1974, many people would doubt that he learned those principles very well. Yet when it came to Native Americans, Nixon did the right thing.

PART 4

Thunder Encounters

*What comes out of dreams can be more accurate than
what you read in the newspapers.*

ROLLING THUNDER

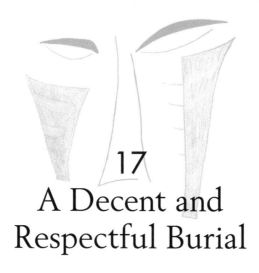

17

A Decent and
Respectful Burial

Michael Neils

MICHAEL NEILS is the CEO of Arize Technologies and president of Solar Generation. He orchestrated Sidian Jones's first sweat lodge in his backyard wickiup, which has hosted Stanley Krippner several times over the years. In retrospect, he summarized the influence that Rolling Thunder has had upon his life.

I transferred to Sonoma State College in 1973, got my anthropology degree there in 1975 and my psychology degree in 1976. It was in Sonoma County that I met Rolling Thunder in 1973 on one of his visits to see Stan. I told RT about my lifelong interest in Native Americans and how, when I was nine years old, I was invited to spend my summer vacation with a Cree tribe in the state of Montana. I returned there each summer and was even permitted to participate in their annual sun dance ceremony. I was adopted into a Cree family and was named in childhood He Who Climbs High Mountain, because of my pastime as a mountain climber.

RT had come to see Stan because there were Indian remains on the territory that was part of the Westerbeke Ranch, the place where Stan and I were living at the time. These bones had been housed in the Anthropology Department of Sonoma State College (now Sonoma State University). RT persuaded college officials to allow him to arrange a decent and respectful burial in the area where the tribe had lived many years earlier. I remember RT remarking, "People dig in our graves instead of asking us what they want to know." Many years earlier, a team from Sonoma State had excavated an old Indian burial site and had removed the bones, placing them in the Sonoma State Museum. RT commented, "We would never dig for other people's bones because it's an amateurish, ghoulish way of going about getting information." That statement certainly made sense to me. And it made sense to the professors at Sonoma State, who took an active role in the reburial.

WHAT ROLLING THUNDER DID FOR ME

RT had a major impact on my life. He substantiated many of my unusual experiences both in the spiritual realm and in the social realm. He gave me the courage to share my experiences with my family, my friends, and my classmates at Sonoma State. They appreciated hearing about the time I spent with Native Americans in their home environments and about some of the ceremonies, like the sun dance, in which I was allowed to participate.

RT never actually shared a dream with me, even though he worked with a number of people's dreams. He was very private about his personal life. However, when I told him about my vision quests, starting with those I had before I met him, he remarked that he had similar experiences in his own vision quests, many of which dated back to when he had been my age.

RT introduced me to a number of Native American medicine men, such as Mad Bear and Shamu. Rolling Thunder also returned to the Westerbeke Ranch many times to gather red oak bark, willow bark, and many other plant medicines that he used to treat the people who, to use his words, he "doctored." For example, he used willow bark to treat arthritis and red oak bark to treat respiratory problems. I continue to use some of the Native herbs that RT told me about. All in all, RT left me a valuable legacy, one that I cherish to this very day.

18
We Know How

Stanley Krippner, Ph.D.

STANLEY KRIPPNER, PH.D., is the Alan Watts Professor of Psychology at Saybrook University in Oakland, California, and past president of the Association for Humanistic Psychology and the International Association for the Study of Dreams. The recipient of several distinguished awards and the author and coauthor of many books, including *The Voice of Rolling Thunder* with Sidian Morning Star Jones, *Demystifying Shamans and Their World* with Adam Rock, *Personal Mythology*, and *Extraordinary Dreams and How to Work with Them*, he lives in San Rafael, California.

Suicide is the second-leading cause of death among Native American individuals who are between fifteen and thirty-four years old. According to the U.S. Centers for Disease Control and Prevention, this is two and a half times higher than the national average for that age group. Overall, the suicide rate for American Indians and Alaskan Natives is the highest among all U.S. citizens, both male and female.

Indigenous people suffer the greatest suicide risk among ethnic and cultural groups worldwide. Young Australian Aboriginal men have a suicide rate four times higher than the general population in that age range. Among indigenous people in Brazil, the suicide rate is six times that of the national average, according to that country's Ministry of Health. This rate is especially high among the Guarani-Kaiowá, who are thirty-four times more likely to kill themselves than are Brazilians in general.

THE ONGOING TRIBAL CEREMONY

I had a personal experience with a branch of this tribe, a group living in the province of Parana, Brazil. In 2011 I attended a conference in Curitiba. The theme of the conference was the many dimensions of consciousness, and I focused my remarks on Rolling Thunder. Toward the end of the conference, a few of us were invited to make a trek into the nearby rain forest for a special ceremony arranged by João Guarani, a shaman for the Eastern Guarani tribe. We entered a dome made of twigs and animal hides and were seated on the ground around a fire. Several members of the tribe began to play drums, and three beautiful, statuesque Native women performed a traditional dance. Once it was over, I thought that this event had certainly been worth our long trip.

But it was not over. Dom João pulled out a huge pipe, filled it with a smoking mixture, took a long drag, and passed it on to me. Wanting to set a good example for the other guests, I followed his example and passed the pipe to the person on my left. After it made the rounds, I felt no effects, but enjoyed the bonding that this ritual had provided.

But it was not over. Dom (a title of respect, corresponding to the Spanish term *don*) João emptied the pipe and filled it with another substance. He lit it, took a toke, and passed it on to me. The smell and taste were different, but also quite pleasant. I inhaled, as did the other members of our group.

But it was still not over. Dom João again emptied the pipe and refilled it, took several puffs, and passed it to me. Again, I followed his example, as did the other members of our group, none of whom were indigenous Indians. I still felt no shift in perception or emotion, but enjoyed the camaraderie.

But it was still not over. Dom João put the pipe aside and brought forth a gourd. He took a quaff of the contents and passed it on to me. I drank from the gourd and passed it on, thinking that this would be a fitting ending to the ceremony.

But it was still not over. Dom João brought forth another gourd, drank some of the contents, and gave it to me. I sipped the brew slowly, trying to identify the taste. Again, it was pleasant and seemed to be an herbal mixture of some sort.

And the ceremony continued with yet another ritual. Dom João took a third gourd, imbibed part of the contents, and once again I followed suit, passing it on.

All of a sudden the six mixtures, alone or in combination, had an incredible effect upon me. My mind was clear, and I thought that I had been blessed by Oxala, the African-Brazilian god of clarity. Nothing I had ever experienced had cleaned the doors of perception so thoroughly—not prayer, not meditation, not LSD, not other psychedelics. The thought passed my mind, *If Dom João could patent this mixture, he would be able to raise his tribe out of poverty with the sales.* Of course, I knew that this was not his way of doing things, given that authentic shamans do not commercialize their magical technology.

But it was still not over. Dom João asked us each to give a prayer. My limited Portuguese has never been as fluent as it was that night. I knew that ranchers and farmers had illegally stolen parts of the Guarani homeland, cutting down trees and turning the land into cattle ranches. Many young people had hanged themselves from the trees in protest. I prayed for the youth to stop killing themselves and conserve their energies for more direct confrontations with the ranchers and farmers who had stolen their land. However, I knew that they had lost confidence not only in themselves but in the magical rituals and tribal myths that had given them their identity for thousands of years.

Dom João gave the final prayer, one that asked the deities to protect us on our way back to our homes. As the members of our group started to leave, the shaman turned to me and asked how I had known about the young people's self-sacrifice. I told him that I was a member of the Rainforest Action Network, a socially active group in the United States dedicated to the preservation of the rain forests of the world. A leader of the Guarani tribe had been a guest at one of our meetings. She told us about the farmers' and ranchers' perfidy and the suicides that were mounted in protest. I told Dom João that the farmers and ranchers could not care less if a few dozen girls and boys gave their lives to stop the destruction of their homeland. Instead, I hoped they would take nonviolent action to save their homeland.

AN IMPORTANT NONVIOLENT PRECEDENT SET BY ROLLING THUNDER

In my limited Portuguese, I told him how Rolling Thunder and his spiritual warriors had stopped the destruction of the pinõn nut trees in Nevada by nonviolent means. These nuts were an inexpensive source of protein for the local Indians. RT's son Buffalo Horse had worked with RT on that project. He had helped the crew of the popular television show *60 Minutes* produce a feature story about it. He also was an advisor for the documentary *The Broken Treaty of Battle Mountain,* directed by Joel Friedman, which had received wide attention.

Buffalo Horse told Sidian and me,

> The ranchers wanted to clear the land and get rid of the pinõn nut trees. They took two big Caterpillar tractors and put chains between them, and when the chains rolled along they would tear up the land. The trees would literally explode. They could clear twenty acres in about an hour. They would destroy so many of those trees that they lined up down the road as far as the eye could see. And nobody was allowed to pick nuts from the trees or use them as firewood. They

would just burn them. This was an insult because piñon nuts are sacred to our people. And you could live on piñon nuts forever if you had nothing else to eat. A piñon nut tree is literally the "Tree of Life."

RT and his spiritual warriors videotaped the destruction of the trees. A few members of his group took the videotape to Washington, D.C., in an attempt to interest important politicians in their need to preserve these trees and their traditional way of life. Their pleas fell on deaf ears, the notable exception being Senator Edward Kennedy of Massachusetts. He knew of President Richard Nixon's interest in Native American rights, and went directly to the White House. The result was a bipartisan effort that stopped the ranchers dead in their tracks. At least for a while.

In the meantime, RT and his spiritual warriors had instituted a delaying tactic. In the dead of night, they poured sand into the fuel tanks of the tractors. The next day the tractors couldn't run and it took several days before the sand was extricated. Shortly afterward, an executive order from the desk of President Nixon stopped the illegal activity completely.

BUT THE ABUSE CONTINUES

Dom João listened intently to my story, much of which had to be translated due to my small Portuguese vocabulary. He said that he would pass on this information to members of his tribe, especially the young people. Since that time, however, outsiders have murdered Guarani activists and tribal leaders who attempted to regain their land. The high suicide rate continues; young Guarani kill themselves twice as often as other tribal youth and six times as frequently as young people in the general population (Lyons 2015). In 1988, a new Brazilian constitution returned land to Brazil's Indians, but farmers and ranchers disregarded it, claiming that it was holding back the country's progress. It is this progress, of course, that has polluted the oceans, contaminated the air, and devastated the forests.

Indigenous people from both continents feel that their relationship with nature is broken when they are separated from their land. In addition to undermining their spiritual base, the seizure of their land has disrupted the social structure of the community. This is shown through more than just the suicide rates; these indigenous people also have a high rate of murder, spousal abuse, alcoholism, and drug addiction. All too often, tribal leaders who speak out against the outrage are beaten, tortured, or murdered. In 2014, Marcos Vernon, a Guarani leader, exclaimed, "This here is my life, my soul. If you take me away from this land, you take my life."

Shortly after making this statement, Vernon was murdered as he attempted to lead his tribe back to their homeland. Survival International, in their November 2014 newsletter, observed that Guarani leaders "are being killed one by one by ranchers and gunmen as a result of their campaign for their ancestral land to be mapped and returned to them." Ironically, the territory stolen from the Guarani-Kaiowá is often used for sugarcane production. Some of the produce is used for alcohol, the substance that, in another form, has triggered its own type of slavery.

The motto of RT's Meta Tantay community was We Know How. Indeed, they did know how to boost their self-confidence, enhance their skills, preserve their communal bonds, and make a positive contribution to their families, their communities, and to nature itself. RT and his spiritual warriors had discovered several suicide-prevention strategies, and they could all be emulated today.

Plate 1. *Owl Medicine* by Duane Red Wolf Miles, © 2013,
www.artoffrequency.com. Owl sees and knows the truth.
When you have lost your way, owl essence will guide
you back to your proper path and wisdom.

Plate 2.
Rolling
Thunder in
Carlin, Nevada.
Courtesy of
Jean Millay.

Plate 3. Wikiup dwelling at Meta Tantay. Courtesy of Stanley Krippner.

Plate 4.
Mickey Hart,
drummer for the
Grateful Dead
rock group, and
Rolling Thunder.
Courtesy of
Stanley Krippner.

Plate 5. Mickey Hart
with Stanley Krippner;
Mickey introduced
Stanley to RT. Courtesy
of Stanley Krippner.

Plate 6.
Rolling Thunder with
Jean Millay. Courtesy
of Jean Millay.

Plate 7. Rolling Thunder holding a baby eagle. Courtesy of Karie Garnier.

Plate 8. Rolling Thunder during a video interview with Jeffrey Mishlove, Ph.D. for *Thinking Allowed,* a program that encouraged the expression of unconventional ideas. Courtesy of Jeffrey Mishlove.

Plate 9. Rolling Thunder and Jeffrey Mishlove, Ph.D., during the *Thinking Allowed* interview, discussing Native American perspectives on ecology and the natural environment. Courtesy of Jeffrey Mishlove.

Plate 10. Rolling Thunder in Germany, where he drew huge crowds to his lectures and workshops. Courtesy of Stanley Krippner.

Plate 11. German edition of Doug Boyd's *Rolling Thunder: A Personal Exploration into the Secret Healing Powers of an American Indian Medicine Man* with RT's inscription for Jürgen Kremer. Courtesy of Jürgen Kremer.

Doug Boyd
ROLLING THUNDER
Erfahrungen mit einem
Schamanen der neuen
Indianerbewegung

Trikont
idianus

To Jorge
Walk in beauty
Rolling Thunder

Plate 12. Rolling Thunder, Stanley Krippner, and Corinne Calvet, a French actress who experienced a successful healing from RT. Courtesy of Michael Bova.

Plate 13. Sidian Morning Star Jones, coeditor of this book and Rolling Thunder's grandson. Courtesy of Sidian Morning Star Jones.

Plate 14. Russell Jones (Sidian's father), Stanley Krippner, Spotted Fawn (Sidian's grandmother), and Morning Star (Sidian's mother). Courtesy of Michael Bova.

Plate 15. Sidian Morning Star Jones, Dr. Larry Dossey, and Stanley Krippner. Courtesy of Stanley Krippner.

Plate 16. Sidian and Stanley receiving the Woodfish Prize from Leslie Gray for their work researching and sharing the teachings of Rolling Thunder. Courtesy of Stanley Krippner.

Plate 17. Sidian and Stanley with the Woodfish group that honored them for their intercultural work that focused on the transpersonal aspects of RT's wisdom. Courtesy of Stanley Krippner.

Plate 18. A group of visitors and friends in Carlin, Nevada. Stanley is in the center of those kneeling and Rolling Thunder is standing fourth from the right. Courtesy of Stanley Krippner.

Plate 19. Jean Millay's portrait of Rolling Thunder in the 1970s, at the time when the Meta Tantay community was being established. Courtesy of Jean Millay.

19
Meeting Rolling Thunder

Tom Eelkema

Tom Eelkema served as a motion-picture cameraman in the U.S. Air Force at Vandenberg Air Force Base, California, and Howard Air Force Base, Panama. He lived in Panama for fourteen years, working as a contract producer for CBS News and Vis News. He wrote us this account of his single but memorable meeting with RT.

I had only one encounter with Rolling Thunder. I attended a talk that he gave in San Francisco in the late 1980s. After the talk, I wanted to have a private conversation with him. It took me over an hour to convince the "gatekeepers" to give their permission. In my fourteen years covering stories in Central America as a contract television producer for CBS News, I have never experienced tighter security. The stories I covered included the Panama Canal Treaty that had been engineered by President Jimmy Carter, an interview with the Shah of Iran, and the final television interview with Manuel Noriega before he was deposed.

In trying to meet with Rolling Thunder, I used every type of persuasive tactic I could think of but nothing worked. Then I said, "I am a friend of Stanley Krippner," and those were the magic words that opened the door.

I remember Rolling Thunder as a very kind person. He seemed surprised that I had so much trouble getting past his security guards. But as I learned during my stint as a reporter, it is easier and safer for security guards to say no than to say yes. However, once I told RT that I was a friend of Stan's, he relaxed and we had a pleasant conversation. I told him that I had interviewed well-known people from all over the world. Some of them left me with memorable comments and some were simply a lot of hot air. Rolling Thunder's comments were a minimum of bluster and a maximum of insight.

20

The Snake and the Salmon

Walter Peterson

WALTER PETERSON received a Master of Fine Arts degree from the Cranbrook Academy of Art in Dearborn, Michigan, and has taught art history for many years. He is a frequent participant in Native American ceremonies. Here is his Rolling Thunder story.

I was attending the Kansas City Art Institute in the late 1960s. My wife of the time was asked by a friend to host a gathering of people to meet and have a discussion with Rolling Thunder, who was described as a Native American medicine man. My friend had met RT at a pow-wow in Oklahoma City and had kept in touch with him. This meeting with Rolling Thunder would be my first encounter with the power of American Indian Medicine, both on a physical and mental level.

Given that this gathering occurred nearly half a century ago, I don't remember many details, but I do recall that it was dark when it started. And I remember that it was a long meeting that went way past midnight.

Rolling Thunder did most of the talking, answering questions and telling stories to all of us. I don't remember asking him a question and

I don't remember the content of his stories. However, what I do recall very clearly is that what he was saying I experienced as though he were talking directly to me, even though everyone else was hearing the same thing. It was like RT was communicating with me on another level. And I felt like I was listening to his stories while simultaneously hearing my mind give answers to personal questions and observations I had.

Later, when several of us discussed the gathering, it turned out that others had this same extraordinary feeling—that Rolling Thunder had been talking directly to them. This was an extraordinary phenomenon that I never experienced with any other speaker I have ever heard.

Another thing I will never forget was the unique ring Rolling Thunder was wearing. It was a coiled rattlesnake made of silver, set with two red stones for the eyes. Much to my quiet amazement, every now and then the snake's head would seem to rise, its red eyes glowing brightly, and the snake would turn its head to look around the room. Then it would settle back down and its eyes would stop glowing. Later when I talked to others who were there, they also claimed to see the snake's head do the same thing.

THE TALE OF THE FLYING FISH

Years later, in the late 1970s and early 1980s, I was teaching at a college in Ashland, Oregon. Bill Lyon, a faculty member in the Sociology-Anthropology Department, brought Wallace Black Elk, a Lakota Sioux medicine man, there for a summer workshop in 1978, which included a series of talks. Black Elk's first set of talks centered on his understandings of the sacred pipe traditions of his tribe.

This initial meeting resulted in Black Elk's return for many subsequent summer sessions, and his talks that second summer emphasized teachings about the Inipi (or sweat lodge) ceremony. One of his "first teachings" was about tobacco ties, also called prayer ties—the small square pieces of colored cotton cloth onto which a pinch of tobacco is placed as one says a prayer. The cloth is then folded and tied onto a cotton string. The intentions vary. Some ties are filled with prayers of gratitude or are prayers for good fortune, whereas other prayers may be seeking guidance from the realm of Spirit.

At the end of one summer session with Wallace Black Elk, I was asked by a friend to go fishing for salmon on the Rogue River. When we arrived at the river, I remembered the tobacco ties, and thought it would be a good idea to make seven prayer ties in gratitude to the Salmon Nation for our success. Once my string of seven ties had been completed, I placed them underneath a rock, and then we walked three miles down the river to a fishing site.

As it turned out the salmon were not active that day and could not be tempted to bite. Very disappointed, we finally sat down next to the river to relax before we started our three-mile hike back. Suddenly the light around me changed, emitting a golden hue in the atmosphere. At that exact moment a salmon jumped out of the river and landed in my lap. I looked at my friend, whose eyes were huge, and his mouth was wide open in disbelief. I then looked back at the salmon and reached down to grab it. However, it was too strong and slipped back into the water. There was no disbelief or thought of my having experienced an illusion because my pants were soaking wet. I also felt the salmon and saw it splash back into the water.

I distinctly felt this was a true gift from the Great Spirit. Consequently, I still give thanks to the Salmon Nation every time I eat salmon.

21
Sensing Rolling Thunder's Energy

Michael D. Austin

Michael D. Austin is a founding manager and strategic adviser who develops companies and hosted radio broadcasts focusing on environmental sustainability, which were syndicated to over one hundred nations. He also works on an archaeological project that has used remote viewing to locate ancient artifacts and a separate project that maintains a private collection of Eighteenth Dynasty Egyptian antiquities. In the following story he shared his recollections of his encounter with Rolling Thunder.

It was at the Healing Light Center Church (HLCC), founded by Rosalyn L. Bruyere, that I watched Rolling Thunder work and got a clear sense of who he was by feeling and seeing his energy. The ability to sense someone's energy was an important part of the HLCC curriculum, and something, once learned, that I have applied in many new encounters. HLCC also was a touchstone for my personal fieldwork, complementing what I was learning at the university and on my own.

Around that time I also met parapsychologist Stephan A. Schwartz (whose account of Rolling Thunder's healing "mist wolf" is contained in Sidian and Stanley's first book, *The Voice of Rolling Thunder,* and is also mentioned briefly in *this* book in chapter 6).

In the early 1980s I finished my bachelor's degree in comparative religion at the University of California, Santa Barbara; environmental studies was my university adjunct field. By then I had been meditating quite a bit, a practice that brought me into quick but deep personal changes. It was while I attended UC Santa Barbara that a masseuse friend introduced me to Doug Boyd's book, *Rolling Thunder.* I loved it and harbored a wish that one day I would have the opportunity to meet Rolling Thunder, although that seemed like an impossibly distant goal. At that early point I'd no idea that my new friend Stephan Schwartz had already seen Rolling Thunder at work.

After I moved to Glendale, California, I spent time with my friends from Schwartz's Mobius Society, and enjoyed this very much. They used "remote viewing" (a type of distant perception) to locate long-forgotten archeological structures, and I found this work fascinating.

I also spent time with members of the Healing Light Center Church that Rosalyn had founded, and was intrigued by her teachings, which centered on healing and intuition (Bruyere 1994). She drew from many traditions, especially and including that of North American Indians. I still have my hand-drawn council fire medicine wheel from one of her weekly classes, showing the four directions.

Rosalyn's teaching suited me perfectly. Because I'm an empiricist by nature, her reputation as the first aura reader, whose experiences were studied in a laboratory by Western scientific methods, helped me be comfortable with her work (Hunt et al. 1977).

THE MOJO OF POWERFUL MEN

When by surprise I eventually met Rolling Thunder, his energy reminded me of Chumash medicine man Kote Lotah's energy, also of the energy of "remote viewer" and military veteran Lyn Buchanan. By profession, these men are all "warriors" through and through. Also a warrior, Rolling Thunder, during his ceremonies, presented an unusually strong presence that simultaneously inspired caution and respect. During the one ceremony that I saw him lead, he clearly wanted to be known as the tough guy running the show. And he got that reception from everyone there.

I can compare Rolling Thunder's ceremony with my experience of His Holiness the fourteenth Dalai Lama. Now, imagine me at that time: a thirty-two-year-old occidental blond man with glasses, in a navy blue suit and tie, sitting quietly in a small reception room at the Newport Beach Country Club in Newport, California. The year was 1989 and I was attending a media reception for His Holiness, which focused on his teachings. This meeting was held during his presentations at Dr. Ronald Wong Jue's Harmonia Mundi Conference of psychologists, immediately before His Holiness would be notified about his Nobel Peace Prize.

During the media reception I felt there'd be nothing I could ask the Dalai Lama that had not already been asked of him. His philosophies were confounding to a Westernized mind like mine, yet were also quite simple. Everyone before me had already asked the same questions that I had read about in the media, so I just listened silently. After the last question had been answered, everyone bolted for the door to file their stories. I was mildly surprised. Instead of rushing out, I waited instead because I thought it was respectful to let His Holiness leave first. I got another surprise when I realized that he had noticed I'd been listening quietly to the proceedings.

He then initiated a bow to me, which I reciprocated as he was leaving. His energy was light, expansive, and welcoming. But it was especially mild compared to the warrior energy Rolling Thunder could flash if he chose.

MEETING RT

It was toward the end of the time I knew the people of the Healing Light Center Church that I met RT. I showed up one beautiful evening at the

HLCC's Alegria Avenue sanctuary in the Sierra Madre Mountains just to see what would be going on. I think it was someone's birthday and I had heard there would be a ceremony of sorts. Rosalyn was part of a group of thirty-five or so people who had gathered outside, beneath the church's square outdoor pavilion. I recall people drumming and chanting. Rosalyn's energy was that of a respectful assistant in the ceremony that followed. Most of the Healing Light Center clan struck me as being fairly sweet people, which was true to the energy of the moment.

Everyone was gathered in a circle when Rolling Thunder entered and walked around it, generally in a clockwise direction. I hadn't known that he would be present and I was pleasantly surprised. But there I stood, several strides beyond the perimeter of the circle, simply watching. This ceremony wasn't focused on any one particular individual I knew, although I did know some of the people in the group. I was thus astonished to feel a distinct presentiment that I would prefer to remain slightly aloof from the circle. Although Rolling Thunder was composed, he was putting out the same energy that any badass warrior would. That wasn't my usual experience of the Healing Light Center tribe. So I watched quietly and respectfully from several strides away, nonetheless aware that the renowned medicine man I'd read about in Doug Boyd's book was now in front of me, working away. In the past, during the Healing Light Center classes or ceremonies, I had often stood at their perimeter as a "dog soldier." In so doing, I was holding space for a successful outcome.

That evening, Rolling Thunder wasn't moving particularly gracefully, as at that point he was no longer a young man. However, although he was showing his age, he still carried as much power and spiritual grace as almost anyone I've ever seen or felt, although I've felt energy as intense as his in only a few individuals I've encountered over the course of my life. It was his strong energy that made me nervous about introducing myself to him.

As he stepped clockwise through the group, there came a point at which Rolling Thunder noticed me standing at its eastern edge. In one of the more curious moments of my life, he looked past everyone—and right into and through me—for around fifteen seconds. That is plenty of time for me to feel what someone's all about. I could feel he was scanning me thoroughly for who I was, and I could tell he was the sort of person who could see anything he chose. You'd expect such skill from someone who, as Doug Boyd wrote, had materialized a tobacco pouch into the backseat of a car from a distant location, even though Rolling Thunder and his fellow travelers had been miles away from that same pouch at the time.

Although I felt his tough-guy energy was unnecessary (it made me uncomfortable), I let him honestly appraise me, without resisting him in any way. However, I was also glad when he turned his focus to someone else. I was simply a casual bystander, and yet because of what I felt from him in that moment, I opted *not* to try and make his acquaintance. I had shown up there to attend a social event and was not in the mood to be tested by or made to fear anyone, for any reason. It was the wrong time and place for me to meet him. But I was very glad and very surprised to have been able to watch him work, and to get some sense of his legendary power.

EVERYTHING COMES FULL CIRCLE

That young man who saw Rolling Thunder working is today known professionally as an entrepreneur, business developer, manager, and fundraiser. I haven't made a habit of talking openly about the healing skills I learned from Rosalyn. In essence, the people of Rosalyn's Healing Light Center represented hands-on coaching and experience that complemented my meditation practice and textual studies of religion at UC Santa Barbara.

At the university, for the campus newspaper, I had interviewed newsmakers. One of my favorite interviews was with Archie Fire Lame Deer, who presaged an impending positive change of attitudes toward caring for Earth. My adjunct field was environmental studies and his words resonated with what I had learned.

Listening to Archie, and after that, having the opportunity to listen to Rolling Thunder speak about respecting Mother Earth, I knew I had truly come full circle in my life. It confirmed my commitment to my current work, which is promoting environmental sustainability throughout the world through the media outreach I do and the companies I found.

22
Let Go of the Shore

Leslie Gray, Ph.D.

LESLIE GRAY, PH.D., is a licensed clinical psychologist in private practice in San Francisco, California. She also studied with Native American shamans and incorporates their traditional practices into her psycho-therapeutic procedures. Dr. Gray's Woodfish Foundation is devoted to integrating traditional culture and Western knowledge. Sidian and Stanley were awarded the foundation's Woodfish Prize in 2007 for their dissemination of Rolling Thunder's teachings. During her doctoral studies, Gray injured her neck in an automobile accident and was still in pain after consulting a dozen specialists. In desperation, she drew upon her own Native American background and visited a Cherokee medicine man, Hawk Littlejohn, whose procedures brought her relief. She asked if she could leave school to work with him full-time, but he told her that although she was called to be a medicine woman she should complete her academic work so that she could help bridge the two cultures. Once she began her clinical practice, she maintained her contact with medicine people, Rolling Thunder among them. She sent us the following account of Rolling Thunder.

Rolling Thunder was a medicine man who had an extraordinary presence in everything he did. He knew how to lay down the law, especially to all those starry-eyed kids with loose boundaries who hung around him. Those rules reflected the way that RT lived in the universe. I think he felt that there were laws to the universe, laws of nature that were central and simple. If you pollute the air, you won't be able to breathe. If you don't take care of the water, you won't be able to drink it. There is a sense of balance in nature, and balance is something that he really understood. Sometimes he didn't want to be a part of that balance, but I don't think he made exceptions to these universal rules. He did often say, "I am not perfect," and he had a terrific sense of humor. For example, he would often comment, "This is the way things go, except when they don't."

In the early 1980s I was invited to do a presentation with him and another medicine man. One thing I remember is that there were a lot of dreamy, long-haired, counterculture people around. I remember one tall, young blond guy with a sweet face who stood up and said, "We've been having a real problem with ants over here." RT spoke right up and said, "The first thing you do is you go where the ants are, and you pray over them. And then if the ants don't go away, you get a pot of honey, and you make a trail from the ants all the way to where the anthill is and leave the honeypot there. If they still don't go away then you kill them because they are pests."

CELEBRATE, DON'T COMMISERATE

Rolling Thunder and the other Elders I listened to told me that we are living through a tumultuous time. But, as I wrote in a chapter for the book *Moonrise,* the Elders also said that this could be a very good time. "There is a river flowing now very fast that is so great and swift that there are those who will be afraid. They will try to hold on to the shore. They will feel that they are being torn apart and they will suffer greatly. Know that the river has its destination" (Gray 2010, 92).

The Elders went on to say that we must "let go of the shore, push off into the middle of the river, keep our eyes open and our heads above the water, see who is with us and celebrate. At this time in history we are to take nothing personally, least of all ourselves. The moment that we do, our spiritual growth and journey come to a halt. The time of the lone wolf is over. Gather yourselves, banish the word 'struggle' from your attitude and your vocabulary. All that we do now must be done in a sacred manner and in celebration" (Gray 2010, 92).

At Meta Tantay, the spiritual community started by RT and his wife Spotted Fawn, there was considerable celebration. RT did not celebrate popular Euro-American holidays such as Thanksgiving and Christmas but he did organize lavish celebrations for people's birthdays. He felt that this would give them a chance to review their past year, let it die, and then be born again.

This is the death and rebirth that I experienced during my shamanic training, and it is a celebration that is available to everyone.

23
Standing Guard

David Sessions

DAVID SESSIONS is a playwright and a native of Berkeley, California. He was born in Roswell, New Mexico, and is the son of the philosopher George Sessions. He and Stanley got together to discuss his encounters with RT over the past several decades.

The first time I met RT I was ten years old. The year was 1973, and my mother and I were driving from Berkeley to Colorado to attend an Esalen conference. When we were near Carlin, Nevada, she took a chance on dropping by RT's house to have, at the very least, an opportunity to give our greetings. But once she mentioned that we were friends of Stanley Krippner, we were ushered into RT's living room and he greeted us very cordially. I do not remember much about our brief conversation, but I do recall his piercing eyes and how they seemed to look right through me.

In 1986, I met RT again. Stanley had invited me to a banquet held in his honor at the California Institute of Integral Studies in San Francisco. The surprise attraction was buffalo meat, something that many of the dozens of guests had never tasted. I was sitting at the same table as Stanley and he told us that buffalo meat couldn't be rewarmed. Once it is ready to serve, it must be eaten promptly or it will become dry and unpalatable. RT was accompanied to the banquet by a troop of young men and women living at Meta Tantay. He seemed to be especially close to one beautiful woman who was sitting next to him at the table of honor. Stanley told her that as soon as the buffalo meat was ready, a university official would give a short prayer, and then she would take RT's plate to the buffet where she would fill it with buffalo meat, potatoes, and garden vegetables. Everything was beautifully timed. Nothing could go wrong. Once the invocation ended, Stanley signaled her to take a plate and proceed to the buffet.

Suddenly, one of the young Indians with RT stood up. "Just a darn minute," he said. "We can't start eating until we've done some singing!" Stanley looked like he had been hit by lightning. He knew that he could not contradict the young brave who wanted to lead the group in song, but he also knew that the buffalo meat was more fragile than the diners realized. He consulted the chef, who told his crew to turn the oven controls down to low for the potatoes and other vegetables. They turned the controls for the buffalo meat completely off. As soon as the singing ended, they turned the controls for the gravy up to high. By the time RT was served, the hot gravy had been poured over the tepid buffalo meat. The vegetables were a bit overcooked but at the right temperature. I could see that Stanley was exasperated, but nobody else knew the difference.

THE FAITHFUL SENTINEL

Three years later, Stanley answered his home telephone. A frantic Mickey Hart told him that RT was close to death from a leg infection. Mickey borrowed a private airplane and a pilot and Stanley met him at the local airport. Together they flew to Nevada, where RT's daughter met them at the airport. Before the end of the day, RT was in a California hospital, resting under the care of Mickey's personal physician.

RT took a special interest in the room next door, one that had a guard posted at the entrance. A hospital staff member explained that the patient was a prominent Mafia member who had been given a temporary release from jail for an operation. The guard was posted to protect the patient from rival factions that might have a score to settle with the ailing godfather. Naturally, RT wanted a guard of his own so Stanley proceeded to telephone friends, and the next day I reported for duty, taking one of several twelve-hour shifts. On that same day, May 31, 1989, RT had the first of two operations that severed his right leg.

I stood guard several times and did my best to keep RT in good spirits. He enjoyed flirting with the nurses and I remember him telling me, "The nurses in this hospital know more about my condition than the doctors!"

On June 1, Stanley and his wife visited RT while I was standing guard. After they left, RT fell asleep and I had to fight from falling asleep myself. Despite my best efforts, by the early hours of the morning I started to drift off into a half-asleep, half-awake state. I don't want to flatter myself and say I had a vision, and I don't remember exactly what went through my mind, but it went something like this.

Thoughts flashed through my brain about the honor of being asked to spend time serving as one of RT's bodyguards. I had been studying martial arts since I was ten and now here I was, guarding a real spiritual master, an influential figure from my youth! But then the images started to shift. I began to consider—whether I wanted to or not—all the ways in which I was *not a warrior*.

What? This really pulled the rug out from under me. I had largely been on my own since I was fifteen. I had climbed the three-thousand-foot vertical face of Yosemite's El Capitan at age nineteen, spending five nights sleeping in a hammock while perched high on the rock wall! And just the year before I had traveled to Buenos Aires, Argentina, to conduct a workshop on martial arts. How could I *not* be a warrior? But according to my inner vision, I was still not a warrior because, truthfully, the recreational drug use of my teens had turned into serious addiction. In my mind I could not become a warrior until I had stopped my dependence on these external substances.

CLEANING UP MY ACT

After the experience of "standing guard," I began trying to get sober on my own but was not having any success. So before long I found myself going to meetings of Alcoholics Anonymous, where I quickly learned that I had to give up any and all mind-altering substances. *All* such substances! I couldn't just give up cocaine or speed and hang on to smoking grass or tobacco from time to time, or even enjoying a single glass of wine. It all had to go.

This was difficult for a young man in his twenties to accept. I was not an old guy in the hospital who had a few weeks to live. As much of an addict as I had become, I still looked very much like a warrior. And yet the more time went by the more it became clear that I wasn't even close to becoming a warrior.

The goal of sobriety continued to become more and more urgent for me, yet I was unable to get clean. As I became closer and closer to admitting defeat and was giving up any hope of dealing with my addiction I discovered there were three hurdles that I needed to overcome.

1. For me, the first and possibly biggest hurdle was to realize there is no easy way to become sober. I had to give up the notion that there was a simple way to do it. I also had to abandon the notion that I could do it in half-measures, giving up some drugs and not others. (Years later, after I was sober, I heard about Jerry Garcia's struggles. Jerry believed that he could keep doing the nonaddictive drugs, like cannabis and LSD, and give up the more harmful substances like cocaine and heroin. But he couldn't stop—or wouldn't stop—and in the end he died of a heart attack while in the recovery center where he was being treated.)

2. The second hurdle was social. I had grown up in Berkeley,

where the people who used recreational drugs were not the *counterculture*—they *were* the culture! All the icons that my friends and I looked up to were using drugs and alcohol. Not only Jerry Garcia and various members of the Grateful Dead, but also numerous other musicians, as well as Timothy Leary, all of whom advocated drugs as a route to creativity. And I truly wanted to be creative. Even Chogram Trumpa, a Tibetan spiritual guru whose books and style of meditation I later studied, turned out to be an alcoholic who drank himself to death, much to the horror of his close friends and followers. And there were several shamans who used psychotropic drugs to get to the "other world."

I learned that RT himself would drink alcohol to excess from time to time and call it "medicine." From where I was standing, one didn't have to look around too far to find the social justification to indulge in such potentially addictive behavior. Many of these social role models seemed to be proud of using drugs and alcohol. Some thumbed their nose at society and at any help or advice that might help them to confront and conquer their addiction. Like Jim Morrison, the sexually liberated and overflowing musician-poet who never admitted defeat and ended up dying in a bathtub, sometimes it caught up with them in the end. This brought me to my third and final hurdle.

3. The third obstacle was the need to admit defeat. And for me this third hurdle proved to be a beginning. Although I couldn't handle the first or second hurdles directly, when I got to number three, I was done.

I was beaten down, underweight, and afraid, and I finally crawled my way into a morning meeting of Alcoholics Anonymous (or was it Narcotics Anonymous? I don't remember). Still high from the night before, I took my seat and listened, ready this time to really take in whatever they were saying. Whatever they had that could help me to never drink or use drugs again, I wanted it! I had been completely and totally beaten and I had finally developed the humility to start fully accepting the teachings and lessons of Alcoholics Anonymous. I worked the 12 Steps. I set aside my old role models and replaced them with new ones. And I stayed sober. For two decades I have been sober.

Perhaps that was my own personal version of a shamanic journey— all of it a result of that fateful night, triggered by serving as a guard for Rolling Thunder while he was recuperating in his hospital bed. The irony is, I thought I was looking out for him. More likely, he had everything to do with *my* healing, and in this, was instead looking out for *me*!

24

He Really Liked the Girls

Oh Shinna Fast Wolf, Ph.D.

OH SHINNA FAST WOLF, PH.D., is the founder and director of the Center for Grandfather Coyote, which teaches Native American healing procedures to healthcare professionals. In 2000, she received the Helen Caldecott Humanitarian Award for Women. When Stanley Krippner was a visiting professor at Sonoma State University, he invited Oh Shinna and Rolling Thunder's son Buffalo Horse to give a presentation to the student body. They talked about the European invasion, the millions of Native Americans who died from European diseases, the displacement of Indians from their native lands, and the numerous treaties that were broken once the United States gained its independence. Stanley remembers that many students began to cry during the presentation, and although the speakers went over their allotted time, not one member of the audience left the lecture hall. Stanley asked Oh Shinna to reminisce about her years as a member of RT's inner circle. Here is her reply.

I met Rolling Thunder through his son Buffalo Horse, with whom I had a long-term relationship. RT was always very cordial to me and

133

often allowed me to witness his healing sessions, or "doctoring," as he called his interventions. Over the years, I observed dozens of doctorings and they all followed the same pattern. First of all, RT interviewed his client, inquiring as to the particular problem that had brought the individual to him to seek his help. These interviews were more thorough than most medical examinations I am familiar with, because RT was interested in the background of the problem and any spiritual issues that might be associated with the ailment. Many of his clients had long-standing problems and RT would ask them about what previous help they had sought.

While the clients were talking, I noticed that RT was listening attentively and also looking intensively. He had a piercing gaze and sometimes it seemed as if he was seeing right through a person. Once in a while, RT told a prospective client that he could not be of help. Usually this happened when an individual had an ailment that was outside of his expertise. RT never claimed that he could heal everyone who came his way. Indeed, if he could not heal someone, he would patiently sit that person down and tell him or her why they needed to find someone else.

When I observed RT at work, I was impressed by how thorough he was. His questions were never superficial, and neither was his advice. He was familiar with half a dozen Native American medical systems, and the trailer where he kept his herbs was filled with hundreds of small bags and boxes, each of them neatly labeled. He even utilized Chinese herbs that had been given to him by Chinese medical practitioners, along with instructions on their use. And more than one Western physician gave him some pharmaceutical samples with clear-cut advice as to their nature and function.

RT AND THE LADIES

It wasn't long after I got to know RT that I realized the he really liked the girls. If he wanted to be with a lady, he would let her know about it in no uncertain terms. He was very direct in making his request. But I never saw him force himself on a woman or use his celebrated status to take someone to bed. If he was turned down, he took the refusal well and did not bring up the topic again. When his offer was accepted it was a matter of mutual consent. Yes, RT really liked the girls. But he never let this proclivity interfere with his work as a healer. And I never knew of any instance where RT told a woman he would heal her in exchange for sex. His private life was one thing. His role as a medicine man was something else altogether. He did not allow them to overlap.

Nor did I ever hear a woman claim that she had been manipulated, bribed, or drugged. Even so, the day came when I had to distance myself from RT. I simply could not condone the way he sized up every new female visitor, wondering if she would be a sexual partner. However, he always treated me with respect and I admired him for that.

UNCONDITIONAL SUPPORT

You might ask what RT thought when I went my own way. He actually supported my decision. He kept telling me, "Never walk in another person's shoes." During the time when I had close contact with him, he kept pushing me to find my own way. I learned many things from RT and put them to use when I founded the Center for Grandfather Coyote, a nonprofit organization devoted to the dissemination of knowledge about Native American traditions, with an emphasis on healing.

RT and I kept in touch by telephone. He would call and ask, "How is my girl doing?" When he called me his "girl," it was done in the way a father would address his daughter.

Looking back over the years, he gave me my independence. This was his greatest gift to me.

25
Rolling Thunder's Medicine Powers

William S. Lyon, Ph.D.

WILLIAM S. LYON, PH.D., is an anthropologist whose book about Wallace Black Elk documented the Lakota medicine man's knowledge and healing abilities. He has also written *The Encyclopedia of Native American Healing* and *The Encyclopedia of Native American Shamanism.* His latest book, *Spirit Talkers,* presents a new paradigm based on quantum mechanics that explains how medicine powers are manifested, which attests to their reality. He wrote us about his memorable encounter with Rolling Thunder.

I met Rolling Thunder only once. It was around 1981 that he made a stop in Ashland, Oregon, where I was teaching at the time. They had reserved a room for his talk at our most elegant motel.

I had been involved with Wallace Black Elk, a Lakota medicine man, since 1978. He had been coming to Ashland annually each summer to conduct sweat lodges and eventually he had started an annual sun dance there, which continues to this day. Also, I had read Doug

Boyd's book on Rolling Thunder. Consequently, I was interested in hearing what this revered medicine man had to say. During my time with Wallace, I had come to meet and befriend Ed Little Crow, a traditional Lakota man who also resided in Ashland. We decided to attend the event together.*

I recall it took place on a sunny afternoon. Arriving a bit earlier than the others we took seats in the front row. Shortly thereafter other people began to fill the room. However, what struck me as a bit odd was that at one point three or four Indian men entered the room; they wore black leather jackets and sunglasses. Rather than take seats, they positioned themselves against the sides of the room. They appeared to be guarding Rolling Thunder.

Being traditionally minded, whenever Ed and I were together, he was silent for the most part and certainly never indulged in chatting. That being said, I had no idea that RT knew Ed from previous visits that Ed had made to RT's Nevada camp. However, those with RT did recognize him, and one man came over and said to Ed, "My dad would like you to join him on the stage." The man explained that Ed would be asked to give a talk, but to "make it short."

Well, when Ed came to the microphone, he started off by telling the audience that he had been asked to make it short, and proceeded to explain that that was not the Lakota way. Then Ed went on to talk as long as he wanted.

I enjoyed both Ed's and RT's talks that day.

THE REALITY OF SEEMINGLY MAGICAL POWERS

I believe what amazed most people who met Rolling Thunder was his ability to wield medicine powers, and I suspect many of the contributions to this book will emphasize that point. He was well-known for his ability to control the weather. I particularly liked reading Boyd's

---

*Ed Little Crow tells his version of the following events in chapter 26.

account of the time RT brought forth a tornado that enabled him to successfully release a Shoshone youth held in the Leavenworth federal prison. Among his many other abilities, RT could cloud his face on a film exposure if he didn't want his photo taken. He could also animate inanimate objects and perform other such feats. At the same time, these are medicine powers commonly displayed by Indian medicine people. Therefore, I would like to honor RT's abilities by henceforth focusing solely on the reality of such powers.

We are educated to believe that stories about Indian medicine powers merely reflect primitive superstitions and illusions. This view has been around since the 1800s. As a graduate student in anthropology, I often wondered how it had come to pass that prior to that time the entire human populace had embraced the reality of magic, usually either in its positive or negative manifestations. But I also asked myself why civilization had appeared to be totally stuck in such an illusion for thousands of years.

The answer is that it isn't an illusion.

Let's go back to the 1800s and the source of the primitive superstition viewpoint. That was the result of a long debate between some of the leading scientists of the day and those who believed in paranormal events and the existence of Spirit. Given that medicine powers are enabled by Spirit, those who believed in their reality were dubbed spiritualists. Some spiritualists were also leading scientists, such as Alfred Russell Wallace, codiscoverer of the process of evolution.

It was a hopeless debate, because there was, and still is, no scientific way of detecting spirits. The evidence put forth by the spiritualists was their direct observations. In fact, at one point the spiritualists convinced one of their leading opponents, Sir William Crookes, to observe their most famous subject, D. D. Home. Among Home's many abilities was the feat of flying out an open window in his apartment and returning through another window. After witnessing this, Crookes reported back to his colleagues that Home's abilities were real. His colleagues were outraged that he was supporting the impossible, and when they voiced their chagrin, Crookes merely replied, "I never said it was possible. I said it was true." In the end the conventional scientists won the debate, but not without lying, cheating, and distorting the evidence.

These scientists claimed that the spiritualists had not provided definitive proof of the existence of spirits, which was true. However, the same scientists neglected to mention that they had not scientifically disproved the existence of spirits. The rules of science dictate that in order to dismiss an observed phenomenon, you must scientifically demonstrate that it does not exist. Until then, you have only a positive or negative assumption—they exist or they do not exist. Thus these scientists treated their assumption as fact, and most other scientists followed along behind the Pied Piper. And just what song was the Piper singing? "We live in a mechanical universe." Well now, that was a flawed assumption as well.

EINSTEIN AND BOHR ENTER THE FRAY

You may remember Einstein's famous quotation "God does not play dice with the universe." Most people don't know what stimulated Einstein to make such a proclamation. It grew out of a debate that arose between Einstein and Niels Bohr in 1927. It was in the fall at the fifth Solvay Congress in Copenhagen that Bohr and his colleagues introduced the notion that observations on quantum-level experiments were influencing the results, which they dubbed the observer effect. In turn, this became known as the Copenhagen interpretation of quantum mechanics.

What perturbed Einstein and evoked his famous quote was that the Copenhagen interpretation put an end to the mechanistic view of reality, a core assumption throughout the entire scientific revolution. Einstein would have no part of a view that entailed "spooky actions at a distance." To that end, Einstein suggested that there was a missing variable in their equations that would eventually be discovered. Unfortunately, neither Bohr nor Einstein lived long enough to see who was correct.

It was not until 1964 that a Scottish mathematician and physicist named John Bell derived a theorem that could be put to experimental test, one that would resolve the Einstein-Bohr debate. It became known as Bell's theorem or Bell's inequality. Interestingly, if Einstein and colleagues were correct, the test would not reveal his hidden variable, only which view was correct. Needless to say, this was a long awaited discovery and met with much excitement. Most of the scientists of that time, including Bell himself, were lined up behind Einstein.

Five years later John Clauser, while a graduate student at Columbia University, conceived the first experimental test of Bell's theorem. Subsequently, he was invited to the University of California, Berkeley, to conduct his experiment, which he performed in 1972. The results were shocking: the experimental results favored Bohr. Needless to say, this discovery set off a series of at least five repeated experiments, both in the United States and in Europe, all with the same results: reality is based on an observer effect. The final test results were reported in March 1999, in an article in the prestigious journal *Nature* titled, "Bell's Inequality Test: More Ideal than Ever." Given the immensity of this change in science's view of reality, some physicists have called Bell's theorem the most important discovery in the history of science. Richard Henry, a Johns Hopkins physicist, views this discovery "to be the deepest discovery ever in human intellectual history." Thus the debate is over. We live in a reality in which consciousness and matter are interrelated rather than in a mechanistic reality, regardless of how "spooky" that may seem.

HOW BELL'S THEOREM APPLIES TO SHAMANISM

One of the most obvious interactions of human consciousness and matter occurs in shamanic ceremonies. It's a simple formula: (consciousness and matter are interrelated) + (humans in a shamanic state of consciousness) = ability to alter reality. This is possible because we exist in a reality that is continually manifesting from the underlying quantum realm that is subject to the observer effect. What we experience as solid actually consists of a host of different spinning packets of energy called electrons, photons, and neutrons. Fundamentally, everything exists as patterns of energy. Medicine powers are simply examples of human consciousness changing those patterns of energy. The same is true of all forms of magic that are not part of a magician's show, deception, or a clever optical effect.

Among Indian medicine people, a medicine-power ceremony entails the participants generating a single, powerful observer effect. This observation is generated through prayers and songs. One often reads of a ceremonial leader asking certain overly skeptical persons to leave before a ceremony begins, the reason being that there is no room for doubt in these ceremonies. Those people who are merely there as curiosity seekers are also asked to leave because any nonbeliever present will weaken the observer effect being generated by those who do believe in what is about to transpire.

The goal of the ceremony is to have all the participants join in one mind and one focus with their thoughts and their prayers. The Naskapi word for prayer translates as "spirit-power-thinking," which anthropologist Frank Speck dubbed "wish power." You put forth your wish in unison, and that creates an environment in which spirits can change local reality. In serious healing cases, one often reads of the ceremonial leader calling for helpers that know how to pray sincerely from the heart. The more prayers you have, the more consciousness input is delivered. Also, given that the intent is to be of a single focus, ceremonies are usually held for only one person at a time. Joseph Eagle Elk, a Lakota medicine man, has spoken to this point (Lyon 2012, 256): "What we had that night . . . was *tawacin wanjila*—we were of one mind, one desire. We did not have two or three patients. . . . No, we had one people. We had one desire. I learned how great power comes when we are one. In my many years of practice, I have not seen the power really come that often. But when it has come, we were all of one desire, one thought locked on the person to be doctored."

This is the basic process by which medicine powers manifest. In a like manner, human consciousness can be used to bring harm, such as the actions of sorcerers or malevolent witches. Nevertheless, the records reveal that a good-hearted medicine person can neutralize the actions of an evil-hearted sorcerer. More important is the understanding that medicine powers are limited. For instance, a patient can be too far gone to be healed. Basically, medicine powers are limited to small changes in local reality, albeit changes that often are quite spectacular. Thus, I would like to give one of my favorite examples of how a group of medicine men working together can achieve an amazing display of power.

REAL-LIFE HEALING EXAMPLES

It is well documented that in the 1800s many different Indian nations held annual medicine-society contests to determine who had the most power. A fur trader named D. D. Mitchell found himself, along with two companions, in an Arikara village along the Missouri River in the summer of 1831 during such a time. They were invited to attend an evening ceremony being performed by a society of bear shamans. Most of the shamans' time was spent in initially modeling small figures from clay, done in total silence, of buffalos and of horses with men carrying bows and arrows. Nine horses with riders were placed together in a line, and facing them, about three feet away, the buffalos were lined up. Once in place, one medicine man commanded them to animate. Thereafter, all the medicine men sat motionless, six feet away, in total silence.

> Conceive, if possible, our amazement, when the speaker's last words escaped his lips, at seeing the little images start off at full speed, followed by Lilliputian horsemen, who with their bows of clay and arrows of straw, actually pierced the sides of the flying buffaloes at the distance of three feet. Several of the little animals soon fell, apparently dead; but two of them ran around the circumference of the circle (a distance of fifteen or twenty feet), and before they

finally fell, one had three and the other five arrows transferred in his side. When the buffaloes were all dead, the man who first addressed [the] hunters spoke to them again, and ordered them to ride into the fire and on receiving this cruel order, the gallant horsemen, without exhibiting the least symptoms of fear or reluctance, rode forward at a brisk trot until they reached the fire. The horses here stopped and drew back, when the Indian cried in angry tone, "Why don't you ride in?" The riders now commenced beating their horses with their bows, and soon succeeded in urging them into the flames, where horses and riders both tumbled down and for a time lay baking in the coals. The medicine men gathered up the dead buffaloes and laid them also on the fire, and when all were completely dried they were taken out and pounded into dust (Lyon 2012, 336).

We are entering a period in which everyone will have to learn to deal with this profound discovery. This includes coming to grips with the reality that our Indian medicine people, as well as all shamans around the world, do indeed wield the ability to change reality simply because the laws of quantum mechanics allow it. This change will be met with as much resistance as experienced during the Copernican revolution, if not more. My colleagues find my new paradigm "intriguing"—because they have no rebuttal—but not convincing enough to change their view.

A GENUINE, POWERFUL PRACTITIONER

I would like to make one final note on Rolling Thunder. It is rumored that he had a gargantuan sexual appetite. I met a young lady in Germany while I was on tour there with Wallace Black Elk and Archie Fire Lame Deer. Subsequently, she came to America to seek Indian wisdom. Her tour included a stop at Rolling Thunder's camp in Carlin, Nevada, followed by a visit to me in Oregon. When she arrived at my home, she told me that she had declined to stay at RT's camp because the staff told her she would have to consent to sleep with RT to remain there.

Take that as hearsay, but what is definitely true is that great power attracts sex in one form or another. Powerful medicine men seem to be like magnets to women. In fact, one of my regular questions when someone tells me about a powerful medicine man they have met is, "How many children does he have?" The more children that individual has sired, the more I'm convinced of his power. In fact, Godfrey Chips, the Lakota medicine man with whom I worked during most of my career, had twenty-three children. So what may appear to outsiders as a sex-driven shaman is most likely a genuine, powerful practitioner.

PART 5

Meta Tantay

We were created to live in beauty.

ROLLING THUNDER

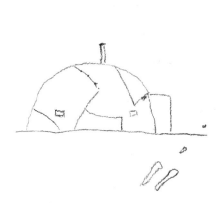

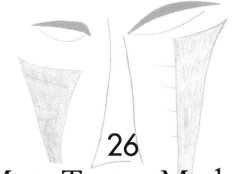

26
Meta Tantay Marked the Beginning of a New Era

Ed Little Crow

ED LITTLE CROW is a Native American activist who was a member of the American Indian Movement. He lives in Oregon, where he is part of the Elders Council, a group that serves Native Americans there, and one that educates non-Indians regarding traditional Native American customs and issues. In a telephone interview, he discussed some of his activities with us.

SCHOOLS AS TOOLS TO BREAK THE INDIAN SPIRIT

I spent eighteen years of my life, on and off, in boarding schools. These schools were part of the government's plan to assimilate Indians, whether we wanted to assimilate or not. I was in about a dozen boarding schools and ran away from every one of them. I would go back to my homeland in South Dakota, where I would usually stay with my grandmother. But then the police would show up and take me back to those terrible schools.

What was so terrible about them? For one thing, they would not let me speak Lakota, which is my native language. Whenever I spoke Lakota, they put lye soap in my mouth and I would taste it for days. In fact, I can still taste it whenever I remember those times. But I never gave up speaking Lakota, and still speak it with anyone who can understand it. The punishment for running away was even worse. They would pour gasoline on my head and would threaten to light it. They would put me in a dark cell with only bread and water for sustenance. I was put in a cell for the first time when I was six years old. But that didn't stop me from trying to escape.

They put us in showers to kill any lice that might be in our hair and then would douse us with flea powder. You might think that this was for our own good, but they treated us like cattle. They would tie us up and douse us with water. They would beat us and punch us with their fists and with sticks. But I was a fighter. I always stood up for the younger boys, so they would beat me the hardest. Why did they treat us so badly? They wanted to break our spirits so that we would assimilate.

I was in boarding schools in Oregon, Utah, and Oklahoma. St. Joseph's Mission School was not as bad as the others but it was still pretty awful. They abused us because they wanted us to submit. They said that it was for our own good. We were given surplus food and Army rations to eat. But we still were always hungry.

When I was with my grandmother, she fed me well. But when I was older, I was sent to what was called a training school. They said this was a "modernized" version of the boarding school. They were supposed to teach us skills so that we could become useful citizens. But it seemed like much of the same abuse and torture. They even brought Indians down from Canada, where they had escaped to. The Canadian government collaborated with the U.S. government to bring Indians back for more assimilation and more punishment. There were many of these training schools on the Missouri River. It was a beautiful setting, but horrible things happened there just the same.

A NEW ERA FOR NATIVE AMERICANS

Once I was out of the schools, my brother introduced me to Rolling Thunder, who invited to me Meta Tantay. I could see that this was the beginning of a new era for Indians. At Meta Tantay, people could come and go as they pleased. They could learn about Native American traditions and history. They were told about the confrontation at Wounded Knee, South Dakota, where Leonard Pelletier was accused of killing two white officers and put in jail. We all knew that the story was fabricated and that the documents were falsified. Leonard escaped to Canada, but the Canadian police arrested him and sent him back to the United States, just as they had returned young Indian runaways in the old days. He ended up in a jail in Florida and the government still won't let him out. Some Native American lawyers continue to work on his case at present.

Today there are many Indian lawyers, doctors, business executives, actors, singers, and everything else you can think of. But they have determined their own future. They have not assimilated. If self-determination had been permitted years ago, many of the problems that Indians face could have been avoided. In my counseling work, I deal with domestic abuse, incest, alcoholism, drug addiction, and all the other troubles that many Indians face each day. I am a member of the Elders Council and we do a lot of service work.

Back in the early 1980s, I went to meet my friend Bill Lyon in Ashland, Oregon. Rolling Thunder was speaking there and I wanted Bill to hear him. RT's son Buffalo Horse came over to me and said that his father wanted me to join him on the stage. This was a surprise but I was happy to do so. RT wanted me to say a few words and I was told to "make it short." The security officers had everything timed down to the last minute. But short talks are not the Lakota way and I gave them more than a few words. The security officers were upset, but the audience seemed to enjoy what both RT and I had to say.

Today I continue my work educating people about Native American ways so that we will never be mistreated again. This is heart-centered work that I am very proud to do, for it is important for Native Americans to understand their true role in history and to be proud of who they are, both individually and as a people.

27

A Memorable Visit to Meta Tantay

Jean Millay, Ph.D.

JEAN MILLAY, PH.D., is a writer, graphic artist, prize-winning filmmaker, psychical researcher, and pioneer in the use of biofeedback in education. Her doctoral dissertation centered on a pioneering experiment in which telepathy was attempted between pairs of intimate friends whose brain waves were being monitored. She is the author of *Multidimensional Mind* and the editor/author of *Silver Threads: 25 Years of Parapsychology Research* and *Radiant Minds: Scientists Explore the Dimensions of Consciousness*. We asked her to recall her one and only visit to Meta Tantay, the spiritual community established by Rolling Thunder and his wife Spotted fawn. Here is her reply.

The Washington Research Institute (WRI) was established in San Francisco, California, by Henry Dakin to advance the study of consciousness. All the psychics, mediums, remote viewers, and the scientists who studied them, were warmly welcomed to it. As a result, many unusual people passed though the WRI at different times from all over the country and various parts of the world. For a while, I was privileged to help organize events at the WRI and to enjoy and study the different realities expressed by the life stories of so many interesting people.

Around 1980, an apartment near the Institute became available, and for a short time a friend of mine named Sola Patricia shared it with me. Not long after that, a medium (who was well-known in the southern part of the state) told us that she had received a message that she should visit Rolling Thunder. The medium asked me how to get in touch with him. I called RT and explained this request. He was reluctant to have strangers come to Meta Tantay; however, he said that if I came with the medium, he would let her come too.

For this story, I shall call the medium Gina, her boyfriend Rick, and his buddy Bob. Gina was used to being the center of attention, and seemed a bit annoyed that RT insisted that Sola and I accompany them. Her somewhat haughty attitude toward us provided us with quiet amusement.

Since the trip would be a long one, I suggested that we camp out the first night at Pyramid Lake. It is a sacred place to Native people, and provides an inspiring environment to the few tourists lucky enough to find it. Its waters flow from Lake Tahoe, which is high in the Sierras and winds its way through the desert of the Great Basin. In these waters, large petrified tufa bubbles, popped from ancient volcanic mud, display their partially open circular forms.

THE JOURNEY BEGINS

Fortunately, Bob had a large van, so the five of us, with our sleeping bags and backpacks, were able to fit in it comfortably. The three of them sat in front and Sola and I settled into the back, and with their CD player filling the space between us, we began our journey over the mountains.

We arrived at Pyramid Lake in the afternoon, found places to put our sleeping bags, and we then enjoyed a gorgeous sunset. Gina and Rick decided to sleep close to the lake, and Bob put his bag down a bit farther.

Sola and I found a soft sandy place between the broken shells of a large tufa, a little ways away from the lake; there we would be out of the wind. We quietly made a smoke offering to the four directions, as well as to the lake. When we settled in for the night, we saw hordes of mosquitoes hovering over us. They seemed to swirl around in order to capture the exact position of our body heat. Just before they descended upon us, bats swooped through the opening of the tufa to feed on them before they could feed on us. This happy arrangement helped us to sleep soundly.

In the morning, Gina complained that some insect had bitten her. Indeed, there was a large, uncomfortable lump on her neck. She was in pain, but she decided that the bite would give her a reason to have RT do a healing for her. We packed up, eventually found a place to buy food to bring to Meta Tantay, and continued our adventure.

Shortly after we arrived at Meta Tantay, we exchanged greetings, and presented our gifts of tobacco to RT, which he accepted gracefully. He also agreed to treat Gina's insect bite—still quite red and painful. Sola was shown the moon house, where she would stay, according to custom for women who were menstruating.

RT chewed some tobacco while one of his "spiritual warriors" brought him a bucket. He began to suck noisily on Gina's neck and spit black liquid out of his mouth into the bucket. As Rick watched, clenching his fists, this went on for some time. RT joked about the sexy noises he made while sucking on Gina's neck, knowing that her boyfriend was becoming more and more upset and jealous all the time. It was pure theater, something fun to watch. When Gina felt the pain diminish, the bucket with the black liquid was buried. Gina gave the impression of feeling that she was entitled to a healing, but RT did not make an issue about her attitude and simply went to work as if she were any other client, not one who claimed mediumistic abilities.

I had heard that there were hot springs on the property and asked if we might go there. The custom was that only the women could go at one time, and that the men would go at a different time. So directions were given, and Gina drove us to a dry area to find a tiny stream of extremely hot water. A small cold stream trickled nearby, and with effort, one could get some of it to run into the hot stream, but very slowly. Gina sat on the bank, deciding that the effort to experience the springs was not worth it to her, but she was willing to wait for me to try it.

I took off my clothes and cautiously stepped into the hot water. Ouch. The amount of cold I could add to this stream was slow and sparse. But I was determined to get into the water, so I meditated for a time to condition myself to be able to stand the heat.

Slowly, I was finally able to sit down in the water. When I did, an astounding thing happened to me. I "saw" on the opposite bank the spirits of many ancient Native women laughing at me because it had taken me so long to adjust. Apparently, the state of mind required to adjust to the heat was similar to that required to become sensitive to the presence of spirits. I will never forget that moment.

When we returned, all the women helped to prepare the food we had brought, as well as the other items that the camp staff added to the meal. Food was carried over to the moon house, where Sola and two others enjoyed exchanging information about their different worlds. Time spent in the moon house was a relief to the women, like a short vacation. Due to the fact that they were menstruating, they were not allowed to prepare food for men or wait on them. The other benefit was that they were encouraged to remember their dreams and tell them to RT in the morning. It was felt that the dreams of a woman during her moon period might provide guidance for the whole group.

AN INTENSE CEREMONY

The next morning, the whole camp gathered on a small hill, where Rolling Thunder led his traditional sunrise ceremony. We all wrapped ourselves in blankets and formed a circle around a large central fire as he offered the tobacco smoke to the four sacred directions. Tobacco was then passed around so that everyone could take a small handful. This ritual offering, RT said, was to be tossed into the fire as we recited our own prayers to "all our relatives." Just in case we didn't know who all of our relatives were, RT began a most impressive prayer. He offered blessings and thanks to all of our ancestors, to all the creatures that walk, and fly, and crawl, and swim—the two-legged, the four-legged, the winged-ones, the ones with fins, and those with many legs. He offered blessings and thanks to the tree people as well.

By then the ceremony was so intense that tears were running down my face without restraint. My heart felt the pressure of opening to all life in the world and to all life in the universe. I could not speak.

After breakfast and bidding warm good-byes to all, we packed for our trip back to San Francisco. Although this was the only time I visited Meta Tantay, it is a cherished and favored memory.

SOME OBSERVATIONS ABOUT
ROLLING THUNDER

In retrospect, Rolling Thunder seemed to be a very talented, yet complex, person.

1. He was an expert on the use of the medicinal plants that grew in Nevada.
2. He told me that if he needed a medicine that he didn't have, he would "charge up" a glass of water with firm intention, and his patient would improve after drinking it.
3. Regarding his theatrical performance during the simple process of removing the insect poison from Gina's neck, he later explained to me that part of any healing is to convince the mind of the patient that the body *is* healing. Because it is the body that actually balances itself into healing, if the patient releases fear, the healing will then be enabled and enhanced.
4. Rolling Thunder's performance in the movie *Billy Jack*, as the elderly medicine man, was memorable. While the film included events in his own life when he was younger, as the medicine

man his speech to the town council came straight from his own understanding of and personal disgust for corrupt politicians.

5. He had a profound understanding of consciousness and the intrinsic connection of all life with Earth and the cosmos.

6. He was, as reported, interested in many women as potential sexual partners. At the same time, he was devoted to his wife Spotted Fawn and spoke highly of her whenever she was mentioned in conversation.

7. He could be described as a recovering alcoholic, and sometimes lost himself to the disease.

8. He often told his friends and his audiences, "I don't claim to be perfect." He never called himself a shaman. He never called himself a guru. He never claimed to be something other than who he was.

28
The Heart of Meta Tantay

Everlight

EVERLIGHT is a spiritual counselor who lives in North Carolina. She combines the energy healing of Matrix Energetics and Owl Medicine with what she has learned from the fields of psychology and philosophy as well as from a study of world religions. Everlight has worked in both the United States and Europe. We asked her to describe Owl Medicine and her connection with Rolling Thunder and Spotted Fawn.

In the 1970s, while staying with Rolling Thunder, Spotted Fawn gifted me with an owl feather, given that I had been very drawn to Owl as a totem. I was then accepted as a family member and was allowed to stay in the family home with Spotted Fawn. Both Rolling Thunder and Spotted Fawn helped me to better understand all of my gifts.

They taught me about "dimension shifts" where Native American Medicine dwells, and how it would show up in my life. They taught me about Owl Medicine as well as the medicine of the eagle, diamondback rattlesnake, butterfly, hawk, and turtle. All these teachings came with many stories. The whole family, to this day, calls me Everlight, the storyteller who brings light with messages. I have shared some of my stories in the 2012 book *The Voice of Rolling Thunder.*

THE WISDOM OF SPOTTED FAWN

When I visited Rolling Thunder and Spotted Fawn, I was also known as Seer and Owl Woman. To those with whom I share messages on Facebook, I am known simply as Elaine Henwood.

Spotted Fawn was an owl person too and was very wise. She was also the very heart of Rolling Thunder's camp, Meta Tantay, in Carlin, Nevada. She kept life running smoothly for her family and at Meta Tantay as well. I trusted her as she trusted me, because she was my spiritual sister.

Back then, I asked Spotted Fawn to share the meaning of the owl feather and the gifts it bestowed. She told me that Owl is a truth seer and bringer of messages. These messages need to be listened to, as they carry a message of truth to those who are paying attention. Spotted Fawn also told me that many people are afraid of Owl because they may not want to hear the truth. She told me stories about how Owl can warn people about an oncoming death, as well as stories detailing how many of these birds have been killed by people who fear death. Of course, this is a wrong label for Owl. It does not cause death, but instead can help you look at your life and find the truth of it before death comes.

But this does not represent the full wisdom inherent in the messages of Owl, who looks through the darkness and sees your hidden secrets and darkest corners. Owl can also bring messages of truth, to help you make changes that you need to make in your life. You may want to hide, but hopefully there will be an awakening of your consciousness so that you can face your problems and make the necessary changes. Owl can also see the light in others and can give many messages of encouragement. You cannot lie to Owl. Instead, you need to listen to its message for you.

OWL MEDICINE AT META TANTAY

There were many, many visitors to Meta Tantay and not all of them came with good intentions. Spotted Fawn said that, as many seers know, we can sometimes be too close to spot trouble when it arises. At that time, a clear seer is needed to help us learn our lessons. Spotted Fawn told me that I could see the source of trouble at the camp and could identify the troublemaker.

Rolling Thunder agreed that one of my gifts was the ability to spot those with evil intent and I was called on a few times for this very purpose. Spotted Fawn said that was why she and Rolling Thunder listened to me. This is why they trusted me and thought of me as a spiritual counselor for their family. He said that my way would be to warn that person that they needed to change—or else! *Or else* meant that their evil intentions would be driven back on them, which would bring about their own self-destruction.

Rolling Thunder and Spotted Fawn also frequently asked me to look into the future for them and for their family members. Sometimes I was asked to give them direction and look into areas that needed work. All of this insight would help each of them travel the good Red Road of Service. For all of the above, I was cautioned that ego should never rule my gifts. To this day, I am very grateful for all of the wisdom and love that Rolling Thunder and Spotted Fawn bestowed on me.

Thank you, Rolling Thunder and Spotted Fawn! *Zon Mea Noh* (Walk in a Good Way).

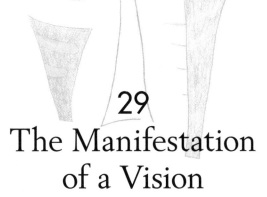

29
The Manifestation of a Vision

Gert Reutter, M.D.

GERT REUTTER, M.D., is a German physician with a private practice in Heidelberg. His specialty is pediatric medicine. He had written to Stanley with a request to find a place for him to study Native American medicine and was directed to Rolling Thunder and Meta Tantay. His experience was a formative one and impacts his practice in many ways, especially his preference for nutritional approaches to childhood illnesses. Here he reminisces about some of his impressions of that time and place.

A friend of mine recommended Doug Boyd's book about a medicine man named Rolling Thunder. This book cast a spell on me, like many similar ones had done in the past. I wanted to meet this medicine man in person and soon was heading for Nevada. When I had finally found Rolling Thunder's small house on the outskirts of Carlin, I learned that several years past he had formed a camp by the name of Meta Tantay. It was located several miles outside of town. I headed for

159

Meta Tantay, and once there was given a place to unroll my sleeping bag.

At the end of my first night under the clear starry sky of the Nevada high desert, I was awakened early for the daily traditional sunrise ceremony. I soon found the cook shack, which was in the central part of Meta Tantay. In the middle of the room stood an older man in a rainbow-colored shirt, wearing a turban adorned with a star made of turquoise stones. This was Rolling Thunder. When I was introduced to him, he shook my hand in greeting. It was a very soft handshake, more of a sensing of my hand. He also made firm eye contact with me, analyzing me as he did so.

THE DREAM OF META TANTAY

I was fascinated with the traditional way of life in the camp and had the opportunity to get to know Rolling Thunder quite well during my time there. Despite the challenging experiences he had undergone as a result of his mixed-blood Native American ancestry, Rolling Thunder had a vision. This vision was the creation of a community where people of different origins, different races, and different nationalities could live together with respect, and in harmony with their environment, or Mother Earth, as he would say. To make this vision come true, he and his wife had bought a piece of land near Carlin and manifested Meta Tantay. This camp was closely tied to him and, despite the fact that it no longer exists, the time spent there was a formative and significant experience for many people, one they would remember their entire life.

To keep the camp running, it seemed to me, was a major effort, perhaps too big of an effort on Rolling Thunder's part. In addition to winding down his job as a brakeman for the railroad, he had to procure the necessary financial means to keep the camp running smoothly, with its myriad activities such as workshops and lectures. In addition, he felt responsible for the welfare and communal life of Meta Tantay's residents—people who had arrived there with high expectations.

To manifest a vision usually takes considerable power and energy. I believe that Rolling Thunder underestimated the effort it would take to realize his vision. Nor did he fathom that the Meta Tantay project would ultimately require too much of him. Spotted Fawn had kept him free of many obligations of the place by her tireless work, but her passing would spell the eventual end of this spiritual enterprise.

IN HINDSIGHT . . .

Many of my experiences at Meta Tantay continue to elude my rational understanding. I could explain them only by way of humanity's original connection with nature and the resultant powers that some people, such as shamans, have developed over the centuries. These powers remain inaccessible to most others and to me. Despite the fact that Rolling Thunder's stories often sounded like literary science fiction, at the time I heard them they sounded authentic. In fact, the feeling often crept up on me that he was able to look around the corner and take a peek into a different reality.

Rolling Thunder was an extraordinary, very complex, and even contradictory human being, with extremely strong charisma. Nonetheless, he preserved his personal integrity and managed to resist temptations that accompany a certain level of fame. He did not want to be—as he would say—a guru. It was important to him that his fellow humans took responsibility for themselves and their lives. What was most remarkable about him, beyond any shamanhood and beyond all the myths that surrounded him, was his profound empathy. He was a person of impressive personal humility and held a deep respect toward all life and all the creations of what he called the Great Spirit.

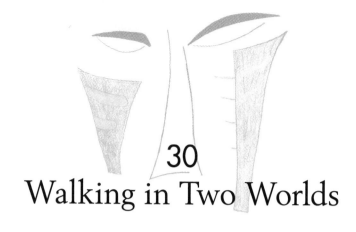

30
Walking in Two Worlds

Jürgen Werner Kremer, Ph.D.

JÜRGEN WERNER KREMER, PH.D., holds a tenured position at Santa Rosa Junior College and also teaches at Saybrook University and Sonoma State University, all of which are in California. He is the editor of the journal *ReVision* and an organizer of the annual International Conference on the Study of Shamanism. We asked him to tell us about his contacts with RT and his wife Spotted Fawn.

Rolling Thunder is among the Native Elders who have shaped my spiritual and academic path. The times I spent with him, both in Germany and in the United States, occurred at the beginning of my ongoing learning experiences with indigenous Elders from several continents and initially he was the Elder with whom I spent the most time. His remarkable example and the provocative questions he raised have led to my current work in shamanism, the recovery of the indigenous mind, and ethnoautobiography. My observations of RT convinced me of the shamanic potentials that are in all of us.

These encounters with RT also alerted me to the often cavalier or mistaken ways in which many nonindigenous followers of shamanism use words that have profound meanings in the cultural practices of indigenous people. RT's charisma and the presence of his healing energy led me to inquire about the traps and challenges of shamanic work in our contemporary world. His Native connections, his intertribal cultural status, and his mixed-blood ancestry made me aware both of my disconnection from my own indigenous roots in the long ago, and the cultural healing work that still needs to occur in the collective.

In this essay, I will retrace the journey of my encounters with Rolling Thunder, from the beginnings at Meta Tantay to his visit to my psychotherapy center in Germany, to the dying of Spotted Fawn and the memorial ceremony in her honor, and, finally, to my last visit with Rolling Thunder in Carlin after Meta Tantay had ceased to exist. Along the way, I will explore issues of healing, creativity, sexual energy, charisma, the loss of Elder circles, and the importance of our ancestries and their indigenous roots.

Rolling Thunder walked between two worlds: the world of his Native origins and the "white" world. Better yet, perhaps he walked in *three* worlds, if we add the spirit or visionary world. His visionary inspiration guided him to enter the spiritual world, yet, at least in retrospect, he had to pay a price for entering this world by being pulled to cater to the black hole of spiritual consumerism and the romanticizing of Native people.

What he has taught me by example are important lessons for anybody and everybody engaged in healing and shamanic work, for sure. However, perhaps more importantly, he also taught me what *not* to do. I am certain he did not intend to guide me to the latter insights, but they were, in fact, inspired by his model. The split of our postmodern world from indigenous roots and connections, as well as the ongoing denials of the continuing destruction of indigenous cultures, create pitfalls for anybody wanting to walk with an indigenous sense of presence.

I have never been a particularly good follower, which I see as a consequence of my cultural conditioning as a German, particularly the lessons from Germany's most recent genocidal history and the impact this conditioning had on my youth. Charismatic speakers have always given me the shivers, not in an excited or pleasurable way, but aversively. I seem to have learned about charisma from Native Elders in a contrarian manner—which has made me no less grateful for what they have given me. Rolling Thunder was always extremely kind, patient, and generous, and I am profoundly grateful for the gifts he bestowed. So when I speak here of the gifts that he gave me unintentionally, I do so with the greatest appreciation for the path he walked and shared.

MY INITIAL EXPERIENCES OF META TANTAY

It was a very cold January. After disembarking my airplane I was standing alone in the Elko, Nevada, airport terminal, waiting for my ride. The hall had emptied except for several Christian ladies who were serving tea, coffee, and cookies as a welcome treat for travelers. After a while they became very concerned about me, and inquired where I was going and who was meeting me. Not knowing the local spiritual politics or the virulence of small-town racism, I decided to be as vague as possible. After a prolonged wait, my ride to Meta Tantay arrived.

At Meta Tantay, I began perusing the faces I encountered until I recognized Rolling Thunder. Aware of protocol, I did not approach him, since we hadn't yet been introduced. Over the next several hours I bumped into him numerous times, without an opportunity for a proper introduction. Finally someone arranged a meeting between us in a trailer on the property. What I most remember is that we were silent for prolonged periods of time. I would look at RT and experience his eyes as gateways or portals through which I could travel into other worlds. I assumed that he was traveling into those worlds himself while he was checking me out. There were no drums or chants. All of this happened quietly as RT was smoking, and perhaps silently making a prayer offering. The subtlety of the situation was in dramatic contrast to romantic images of wildly dancing Plains Indians that I had grown up with.

This encounter was the beginning of a relationship in which I always felt welcome to come and visit, bringing my questions and concerns into our conversations as RT was sharing his insights and teachings.

I had grown up in Germany with a deep connection to the forest, the moor, the sand dunes, and the river marshes that surrounded my family home. However, I found the invasions of the surrounding industrial society relentless and profoundly disturbing. My time at Meta Tantay allowed me to develop at least a faint sense of indigenous presence in a particular landscape or ecology—with the interstate and railway as backdrop. The sunrise ceremonies that RT held taught me what Native presence, responsibility, and connection to the land might look like. The experience of the cold was part of this sensing, as was the perception of energy emanating from the hands that held tobacco offerings in prayer in the freezing cold as daylight intensified. I also found the song of the sunrise ceremony very moving. It was imprinted on me so clearly that, to this day, I remember it well enough to sing it.

I began to feel embedded in the vast landscape of Western Shoshone lands in what is now the state of Nevada. The mold of the land started to enter my brain and I began to draw numerous images of Meta Tantay reaching into the surrounding landscape. These were not so much realistic drawings as they were sensed impressions of juniper trees, valleys, creeks, hills, washes, and mountains reflecting at least a *faint* sense of my remembered native presence in the landscape.

During my time at Meta Tantay I stayed in a wickiup. I had to keep the stove going all night in order to stay warm enough in my sleeping bag. One morning I was roused at 3:00 a.m. to leave my comfortable spot and join the lineup for a sweat-lodge ceremony. This was my first such experience and it bonded me to this form of prayer, song, and purification. The ceremony ended before the sun was up. When it was over, I crawled back into my sleeping bag until it was time for the sunrise ceremony.

In a number of conversations over the next few days, I made the necessary agreements with RT for his visit to my psychotherapy center in Germany.

THE NATURE OF CHARISMA

RT's visit to Cologne, Germany, was a great success. He first held a press conference and then gave a wonderful workshop with Stanley Krippner. The grand finale was a lecture to more than a thousand people in a large hall in Cologne. The admiring and even romanticizing relationship between many Germans and Native Americans, particularly the Plains Indians, is legendary. I observed and reflected on the dynamics of this as they unfolded in the lecture hall, which was filled to overflowing. RT's charisma surely carried the evening and his audience was moved and inspired.

I started to speculate about the process of charisma—its impact on the person with the charisma as well as the people impacted by that person's charisma. It occurred to me that there are two forms of charisma that, while distinct, are not always neatly separable. I called one type of charisma *natural* and the other type *inflated*. I realized how easily natural charisma gets pulled into the dynamics of inflated charisma through the social forces of money, fame, romanticism, spiritual hunger, and more.

By *natural charisma* I refer to human beings who live close to their natural gifts, and who are psychologically and spiritually balanced enough to allow their gifts to shine. This would be a result of their upbringing, culture, and inner and outer work. They have been raised, or trained themselves, to live close to their essence or their medicine, so to speak. This is what makes them attractive, beautiful, powerful, and inspired in the perception of the audience.

By *inflated charisma* I mean a style of presentation and leadership that implies a dialectic process of deflation with the audience or followers. Oftentimes, this involves a process of mutual flattery that empowers the charismatic speaker and disempowers the followers. This dialectic facilitates a meeting of unresolved psychological patterns in both the charismatic leader and his or her audience. It amplifies them, but does nothing to resolve them.

While natural charisma has nothing to do with any visibility in the public eye, inflated charisma *is* created by public visibility. Potentially old patterns of personal or collective wounding may become activated in this process and the connection with one's medicine and "healing gift" (to use the common parlance of Native American terminology) may weaken or become redirected. The result may be ego inflation. Inflated charisma may also strengthen one's defenses against shadow material, whether personal or collective.

CHARISMA'S IMPACT ON RT'S GERMAN AUDIENCE

How did all of this play out in Cologne when RT was speaking in front of a large audience hungry for his message? The disconnection from indigenous roots and presence has a long history in Germany. Most recently, Hitler—to promote his genocidal purposes—abused the mythic stories that had emerged from ancient practices of being embedded in nature and attending to spirits. As RT mentioned during his Cologne lecture, at one time in Germany's history, witch hunts had exterminated the shamanic practitioners who retained indigenous healing knowledge, specifically midwifery and herbal healing. And looking farther back, the rise of Indo-European patriarchal systems had split people from the ancient wells of memory and the trees of life that had been at the center of Germanic indigenous life and understanding. These disconnections can be understood as a dissociative cultural trauma that results in both a powerful shadow (the violent aspects of history) and a tremendous spiritual hunger because the old sources of life renewal were no longer accessible.

This hunger for Earth-based living was easily projected onto RT's presence, his natural charisma serving as a catalyst for the desire to reconnect with an Earth-based philosophy. And I fear this led, in some members of the audience at least, to an increase in what has been called the "romance of Natives," for which Karl May's translated adolescent novels of the Wild West had prepared the ground.

Sadly, this projective and deflationary process would prevent many of the Germans present at RT's lecture from looking at their own ancient cultural practices, which were capable of feeding this spiritual hunger instead. Looking toward an idealized and inflated Native American image also avoided the confrontation of traumatic barriers—the shadow of the dissociations from European indigenous practices. I fear that the number of sincere and well-intentioned "German Indians" might have increased instead.

Some Native Elders moving between cultures, such as Apela Colorado, Leslie Gray, John Mohawk, Vine Deloria, and Ward Churchill, have spoken of the necessity for all people to remember their *own* ceremonies. This recall allows us to visit each other's ceremonial fires again in indigenous exchanges of celebration and knowledge. Rolling Thunder's *natural* charisma clearly inspired and roused the audience, but I wondered where they took their newly kindled inspiration and how they parlayed it in their own lives. His critical statements about the destruction of Native people, the destruction of nature, and the need to pay attention to Mother Earth were an urgently needed message. The enthusiastic response it received showed how welcome it was.

ADDITIONAL IMPACTS
OF ROLLING THUNDER'S TEACHINGS

The tremendous success of RT's appearances in Germany made me critically aware of the market dynamics of fame, notoriety, and money. RT was frequently on the road to spread Native American teachings and to follow his vision, for sure, but he was also under pressure to sustain Meta Tantay financially. Given all of these considerations, I came to the conclusion that it is very difficult for a person with natural charisma not to get seduced into dynamics that led to an inflationary dynamic of charisma. This is because making money and being in the public eye usually mean that people have to sell their natural charisma in such a way that the inflation of their charisma, with a concomitant deflation of those who spend their money to listen and follow them, seems almost inevitable.

I have observed on numerous occasions this dynamic of *in*flating the worth of one person while *de*flating the level of self-empowerment, self-love, self-assertion, and self-acceptance in the audience. Oftentimes this is done with the help of an ideology or philosophy that promises the opposite by using the language of empowerment. This creates a double bind: The spoken message is empowerment, the unspoken message is disempowerment (*inflationary* charisma fueled by the uncontained projections of followers), and there is a prohibition against raising this contradiction to the level of discursive awareness. It seems that this dynamic becomes particularly virulent in the realm of spiritual work; the spiritual hunger and the trauma of disconnection from the sources that feed indigenous presence seem to give it an extra force or intensity. It appears that inflationary charisma strengthens or amplifies whatever imbalances, unresolved issues or latent pathologies an individual carries. On the other side of the dynamic, spiritually starved and hungry followers are usually loath to see such latent or even blatant pathologies. Such imbalances and even pathologies nonetheless have to be understood in terms of the spiritual goals and the integrity any spiritual path and leader espouses. I regard my increased attention to this issue as a gift from RT, whose presence sharpened my own sense of psychospiritual responsibility.

I never had the opportunity to discuss any of this with RT and I have often wondered what his personal experience of it was while he was in Germany. I know that he always "doctored" himself spiritually before these public events and I assumed that this was, at least partially, to protect himself whenever he put his charisma onstage, front and center.

THE OBJECT OF MY DREAM

Once I had moved to the San Francisco Bay Area, I visited RT in Nevada on an irregular basis. One night, at my home, I had a dream about a ceremonial item that had been fashioned from various objects.

Most of these objects seemed to be from the sea—for example, shells and sea urchin spines. In the dream, this object was placed on my altar. I remembered the dream clearly and wondered about the meaning of the object.

Soon thereafter I went to the Jump Dance on the Hupa reservation. During one of the breaks I walked into a crafts store and had a déjà vu experience. As I entered the building everything seemed strangely familiar, and it was as though I had been there before. My state of awareness seemed to be altered. Perhaps this was an intensification of the mild trance I had entered while watching the dance. As I looked around at this surprisingly familiar world I saw all the different parts from which the altar object of my dream had been fashioned. I began to gather the pieces together with the intention of fashioning the object myself, which I did upon my return from the ceremony. After that I lived with the object on my altar for a few months, where it became the focal point for my meditations and visualizations.

The next time I visited RT I took the object with me to ask him about it. I told him the dream and the subsequent events in Hupa land. He didn't give me any interpretation, but he said that he would remember it and would work with it ceremonially, saying "I will take care of it." RT then completed the energetic movement when I left the object with him. Here any intellectual interpretation of the dream object was disregarded in favor of the shamanic energetic movement, during which the veils between my dream world, the visionary ceremonial world, and my daily life had been thinned. Instead of looking for cognitive revelations, the action and embodiment that resulted from the dream became important.

Paula Gunn Allen (Allen 1998, 47) noted, "In tribal cultures, ecstatic, mystical states don't so much convert into emotive personal experience as into physical experience or experience with direct effect in the physical (that is, as a consequence of entering an ecstatic state, a practitioner can do something actual)." For example, if a flicker bird appears in your dream, then it may not be so important to interpret the meaning of the flicker bird as a symbol, but to go out and see if a flicker appears in real life and to observe it—or to embody flicker energy. It is the energetic movement throughout the different aspects of consciousness and awareness, the practice of thinning the veils, and the nimbleness with which we integrate visionary experiences with our daily lives that matter.

RT never revealed to me what he did with the object, but this is what I took from his response to my dream. Since then, whenever a dream gives me ceremonial guidance, I take it very seriously and follow it to the extent I can. Rather than relying on an intellectual interpretation, I sense the energy of the dream and attempt to follow the movement as it impacts my daily life.

31
Healing from Creation

Jürgen Werner Kremer, Ph.D.

JÜRGEN WERNER KREMER, PH.D., holds a tenured position at Santa Rosa Junior College and also teaches at Saybrook University and Sonoma State University, all of which are in California. He is the editor of the journal *ReVision* and an organizer of the annual International Conference on the Study of Shamanism. We asked him to tell us about his contacts with RT and his wife Spotted Fawn.

THE CHALLENGES OF BEING A HEALER

When Spotted Fawn was dying, Stanley Krippner took me along for a visit to see her at Letterman Hospital in San Francisco's Presidio district. He had been making periodic visits to her bedside to ease her pain through the use of hypnosis and mental imagery. Despite her illness, she looked tremendously beautiful. RT asked Stan to work on Spotted Fawn and he did some of his own medicine work at the same time. It became clear to me how difficult and challenging it was for RT to let go of his wife. His language beseeched her not to cross over to the other side. He remarked, "Her relatives are calling her, but I am telling her not to go there." His natural ego attachment to his wife, I believe, got in the way of the healing work that needed to happen, (which seemed to me would have been helping her to transition, rather than keeping her alive despite what clearly was a terminal illness).

The challenges of a healer working with family members are not dissimilar from those of a psychotherapist working with friends or family. The healer is challenged to enter and surrender to the spiritual process of creative healing energy. While this takes intention and focus, our ego attachments can limit the options and prevent grace from entering. Needless to say, if I had been in the same situation I would have gone through similar struggles with my attachments, of course with much less confidence regarding my healing capacities.

It's in situations like this that I feel the consequences of the Native American genocide most intensely: Where were RT's peers when he needed them? Where were the Elders to support him? The loss of Elder circles struck me as tremendous and made Rolling Thunder's road seem ever more precarious. I had met Keetowah, a Cherokee Elder whom RT regarded as a spirit brother. During my encounter with him I had an impression of similar traditional visionary depth. RT felt that he was guided by the seven stars in the Pleiades constellation and he would often wear a turban with a seven-pointed star on it. He felt especially close to those who were guided by the same stars, and Keetowah remarked that he felt like RT's twin because of this Pleiadan connection. But beyond what seemed to be more isolated encounters, there also seemed to be many deep scars that had been left by the devastating history of white/Indian interaction. In the face of this, however, RT persisted with his inspiring message without the reliable support of and connection to a community of Elders.

WHAT'S REALLY HAPPENING IN THE HEALING REALM

My observations of Rolling Thunder, my observations of other indigenous healers, and my own accidental and intentional experiences with alleviating the suffering of others have led me to a particular understanding of healing. Stanley Krippner has described a persuasive quantum theory of healing in his book *Realms of Healing* (Krippner and Villoldo 1976) that still holds water. My own language is much more informal and inspired by Native American traditions, conversations with healers, and my own cultural background.

The Native American healers I have come to know, including RT, frequently stated that it was not they who did the healing but Spirit, or the Great Spirit. In this sense, the work of the healer connects with energies that are beyond our common awareness, energies that heal or are creative in the sense of helping a person to find balance and health. This model of energies may appear to be somewhat Western, but on occasion, I was privy to similar and lengthy explanations about different energy levels, for example during a sweat-lodge ceremony on the Navajo reservation. The challenge of any healing intervention is to generate the necessary *creative* energies so that Spirit (or the spirits) may intervene; some people call this grace. The gift, training, and presence of the healer help to make an extra amount of energy available that may jump-start the inner self-healer of the person suffering. It's also important to understand that healing does not necessarily happen because of one person, but because of the healer's connections with Mother Earth, spirits, the Great Spirit, ancestral spirits, and other "relations." The healer is able to connect the person suffering with this much larger, more universal process known as the spirit world.

The closer persons are to their essence or medicine, the easier it is for them to access and catalyze these creative energies. The catalysts may be drums, chants, medicine items, a Tree of Life, herbs, hallucinogens, dancing, or fasting, for example. Each tribal tradition seems to have its arsenal of techniques and technologies to facilitate the access to the spirit world of Creation for the sake of healing.

When Rolling Thunder talked about healing he was always discussing his own gifts, it seemed to me, in the context of this much larger process. He felt very confident about his capacities, but he always placed them in the context of the larger circle.

It is my belief that when RT was "feeling" me during my first encounter with him, he was doing exactly that. As discussed, I experienced this subjectively as portals opening through his eyes and I could sense the other worlds he was roaming in order to determine whether or not he could connect with me through them, and whether or not I was trustworthy enough to host him in Germany. I could sense this through his eyes, almost ready to travel with him. All the while RT was smoking his pipe, filled with the ubiquitous Five Brothers tobacco.

Later, at the press conference for RT in Cologne, a baby's hand was caught in the door and she was crying with intense pain. RT walked up and touched her hand for a short period. The baby stopped crying and was comfortable for the remainder of the press conference. Because RT was a gifted healer he could instantly tap in to that spiritual world of creative energies that were readily available to him. His training and deep connection with the community of nature (whether his Rattlesnake Medicine, or the coyotes, or his various healing plants) allowed him to open the doors to healing energies not just in more formal ceremonial settings, but also in everyday settings without any ceremonial to-do.

During one of the hospital visits with the dying Spotted Fawn, Stanley was asked to use his own hypnotic imagery work to help her. Here Stanley used the power of the imagination to tap into the creative and healing realms to relieve Spotted Fawn's suffering. He entered the imaginal realm using standard psychological techniques that connected him to these creative energies. Stanley's clear focus and intent were appreciated by Rolling Thunder and Spotted Fawn, for they had a positive effect on her.

As horse and other animal whisperers report, animals communicate in images, not language. Command of the imagination connects us with deeper structures in our brains, structures that are important in dreaming and trances. Creative energies inside of us, whatever their source, seem to manifest through these older mammalian brain structures. We might say that imagination is in service of creative energies and of the imaginal or spiritual realms, while fantasy is used in defense of creative energies and prevents the emergence of an authentic and grounded sense of self.

After Spotted Fawn's passing, a memorial ceremony was held at Meta Tantay. It was an amazing, albeit profoundly sad event. The feast in her honor was tremendous and the buffalo meat that slowly cooked in a pit for the better part of the day was the juiciest and best I have had. Rolling Thunder talked at length, and during the ceremony I saw an image of Spotted Fawn's beautiful, large face, now much, much larger than life-size, hovering over the gathering. It was a beautiful and moving memorial.

PRIMAL ENERGIES AT PLAY

The term *creative energies* finds a particular expression in the Navajo understanding of healing. Hanson Ashley, a roadman or ceremonialist of the Native American Church, talked to me about the ritual movement in Navajo chantways. In this understanding, patients need to return to their origins from Creation so that they can be re-created in balance and health, so that their story can be remade and retold in beauty. In chantway ceremonies the person being healed literally gets placed on the sand painting, at the point designated on the painting to be the point of Creation, so that he or she can be re-created ceremonially and in balance, from the source or the origin.

The chantways are designed to help Navajos "walk in beauty on the road toward old age." The ceremonies generally entail at least one of the following elements: chants, masked god impersonators, dances, purifications, prayer smokes, and more. During the three to nine days of ceremonies the person to be healed and the other participants consistently evoke the spiritual realm of creative energies as night becomes the ceremonial day and sunset marks the beginning of the liturgy, engaging everybody in the local web of nature and its gods.

Creative energy also manifests in humans as sexual energy, leading not just to pleasure, but potentially also to confusion and abuse. The sexual stories around healers are legion, as are the suspicions of improper sexual proceedings during ceremonies. The Old Norse *seiður* ceremony, a ceremony in which the energies are brought to seething (seiður), has often been dismissed because of suspicions about its sexual nature; and men performing seiður were discriminated against as being gay. But sexual energy, as many healers have attested, is part of the manifestation of creative energy. The Sámi *noaidi* ("seer" or "shaman") Ailo Gaup told me how he at times would get sexually turned on during ceremonies and healings. Sexual energies are the part of creative energies that we have the easiest access to and that allow us the simplest way to translate them into behavior. I would suspect that the perception of creative energies as sexual is the known and more comfortable aspect, while other aspects of creative energies are more mysterious and thus less easily perceived. Frequently participants in ceremonies have commented on the raised level of sexual energy in ceremony and their openness to it.

In Old Norse mythology we have Freyja, who acquired one of her central shamanic emblems, the *brisingamen*—a necklace with shamanic powers—by having sex with the dwarves. Similar to Siberian traditions where the shamans depend on the smiths to create the necessary shamanic tools, here the shaman goddess Freyja is dependent on the dwarves who work the earth's minerals and metals (just as we find as a remnant in the story of Snow White and the Seven Dwarfs). Freyja's sexual concourse with the dwarves was an energetic exchange for the sake of acquiring healing powers, one where no moral concerns apply. Her mastery of creative energies was the focus, and enabled her empowerment as a shaman.

NEGOTIATION AS AN ESSENTIAL SOCIAL MECHANISM

Rolling Thunder often talked about the agreements that Natives made with the game they wanted to hunt, how other things were negotiated, agreements were made, and obligations for certain behaviors were agreed upon. This negotiation and prayer were necessary to keep everything in balance. Although I have heard this process referenced by a number of Native American healers, I had never heard or read a very detailed account of such a negotiation or energy exchange until I found Willerslev's description of this (Willerslev 2012). The following is an example of the generation of creative spiritual-sexual energy, not for the sake of healing but to provide sustenance through hunting.

The Yukaghir Elder Spiridon is not called a shaman, but is a hunter who lives in a shamanic universe, clearly connected with one of the old Siberian traditions. The story is stunning in its shift of patterns of phenomenal properties or worlds, and in the energetic and real world results that different attentions yield. Yura is Spiridon's son and they, including the anthropologist Rane Willerslev, are out in the Siberian taiga in the depths of winter with temperatures dropping to minus 70 degrees Fahrenheit and further. Yura urges Rane to get the move on since the Big One is near (*Big One* is a euphemism for moose):

"What on earth were you talking about?" I ask Yura.

Yura thinks for a moment. "How should I explain it to you?" Then he reaches down into Spiridon's [the shamanic hunter's] sleeping bag and pulls out a little wooden figurine. It has the shape of a crudely carved human body, with lines marking eyes, nose, and mouth. Something resembling moose antlers have been carved on top of the head. "This is my father's *ayibii*, or what the Russians call a soul (Russian, dusha)," Yura explains. "During the night, it goes to the owner of the River Omulevka. She lives in a house with a big stall. All the animals live there—when they're not running round in the forest, that is. She loves Dad, and they have . . . "

Yura stops for a moment and laughs. Peter laughs with him.

"What?" I ask impatiently.

"Well, they have sex with each other."

"But why do they do that?" I am quite dumbfounded.

"Because then the Big One comes running all by herself" (Willerslev 2012, 106–107).

After hiking for four hours through the snow the old shamanic hunter steps into action.

Spiridon points to a track in the snow. He does not say anything but signals that we are to stand still. He himself continues out into a clearing some few yards farther forward. He waddles back and forth on his skis, and his body has taken a new shape. He no longer appears like an ordinary man. The fur jacket worn with its hair turned outwards, the fur hood with tassels of moose ears sewn on, and the fur-covered skis all make his movements look rather like those of a moose. And yet his human nose, eyes, and mouth can be glimpsed under his hood. In his hands he holds a loaded rifle.

Suddenly a cow moose steps out of the brush, along with her lean, long-legged calf. At first the two animals stand still, while the mother lifts her enormous head with its long, pointed beard up and down in evident confusion about what kind of being is approaching. But as Spiridon gets closer, she is seized by his movements, sets her mistrust aside, and runs straight toward him, with the calf bounding after her. In the same instant, Spiridon lifts his rifle and kills both of them with a volley of four shots.

I stand gaping as I watch the whole scene, which seems completely crazy. Yura nudges me in the side: "That's what I said, the Big One comes all by herself" (Willerslev 2012, 107–108).

As attention shifts, the objects of consciousness shift from sex with the female spirit keeper of the animals to mundane activities of preparation, the hunter shifting attention, the phenomenal properties of the world of the two moose, and their killing. The hunt emerges from the generation of creative, sexual energies, the energies manifest from the world of spirits in a successful hunt, which means food on the table. It is dramatically different from any mere cognitive or emotional interpretation; the work with creative energies had an effect in the physical world.

While this story is truly extraordinary, if we look at it from the perspective of attentional shifts resulting in different patterns of phenomenal properties, then we normalize the experience and have the opportunity to remember it as human potential. Indeed, it challenges us to question our notions of reality, as Willerslev does in analogous language: "We cannot, therefore, simply relegate dream content and meanings to the interiority of the unconscious mind. . . . Whether one is awake or asleep, a person's encounters are always those of being-in-the-world and never an empty reality. . . . The awareness of the dreaming self is as phenomenally real as when the person is awake" (Willerslev 2007, 180).

Willerslev concludes that the "conventional discrimination between the 'natural' and the 'supernatural,' the 'real' and the 'culturally constructed,' cannot easily be maintained. We will no longer be able to hold that conceptions of animal, trees, and mountains are more real than those of spiritual beings" (Willerslev 2007, 210).

THE SPECTRUM OF REALITIES

The worlds of dreams, shamanic visions, and other experiences can find their place among the spectrum of realities. As Krippner (2004, 210) wrote, "Any product of human imagination represents a form of reality." Our shifts in attention lead to different patterns of phenomenal properties or realities—and who is to say which one is more or less real?

RT certainly walked with ease between the worlds and he was able to focus his attention both on the community of the natural world as well as the Spirit world of creative energies with equal ease. One was as real to him as the other and he was able to use the training and gifts he had received, whether from Rattlesnake or conversations with Coyote, for the benefit of others.

THE GIFTS HE LEFT BEHIND

At the time of my last meeting with RT, Meta Tantay was defunct and it was not long after this visit that he passed on. A Swedish friend of mine and I visited him at his house and he talked at length about healing and his use of herbs. While he clearly wasn't very well, the conversation was like many good old times we had shared before. We camped on his property in Carlin and honored the sunrise in ceremony the next morning. A young woman who was taking care of him led the ceremony; RT was not present. During our leave my car was ceremonially blessed with tobacco and a bag of it was tied to the front of the car. It stayed there far beyond the return trip from Nevada to the San Francisco Bay Area and lasted more than two years. I was grateful for this visit, poignant as it was.

Rolling Thunder opened an important door for me. He showed me how we are embedded in nature, and he taught me about our ecological grounding and the community of plant, animal, and Earth spirits that surround us. He taught me that the healer never heals, but that it is the work of the Great Spirit (or grace or creative energies). He taught me about humility. From him I started to learn about the importance of energetic or spiritual movement (rather than emotional or cognitive responsiveness and interpretation).

The beauty of Meta Tantay has imprinted itself in me as a guiding principle for the work to be grounded in the particular place we live in. Without RT's example, I would have never dared to jump into my first healing endeavor. And he made me a garlic lover. When he stayed near me in Germany, the kitchen literally reeked of garlic when food was prepared, a testament to its alleged healing powers.

Beyond the things I learned through conversations and ceremonies with RT, I also learned about spiritual dangers. In the charged charismatic cycle necessitated by the needs of the Meta Tantay community there was no space to acknowledge all the intricacies of personal history and mixed-blood ancestry and the obvious need for cultural healing.

The lack of an Elder circle represented a continuation of genocide and prevented the support that RT deserved, as did all of the other isolated Native Elders.

Over the years, I have continued my work with Native Americans and other indigenous shamans, Apela Colorado in particular. In so doing, I have come to the conclusion that the complexities of our ancestry matter tremendously for personal and cultural healing. I am following RT's call for cultural change through my own work of ethno-autobiography (Kremer and Jackson-Paton 2014), an indigenous-based approach designed to help students remember their ancestral and indigenous roots. RT frequently talked about contemporary social problems, the history of genocide, and the misguided philosophies presently at work. I am committed not to separate any healing work, psychological and otherwise, from the cultural healing work and the recovery from generational traumas and dissociations. We do need to remember and recover our own indigenous mind and wisdom.

My understanding of the dynamics of charisma has led me to the development of twenty-five meditations that bridge the personal and psychological with the spiritual and cultural (Kremer et al. 2001). I have come to use the Andean phrase *criar y dejarse criar* to introduce each meditative statement; the phrase evokes my experience of embeddedness in the landscape of Meta Tantay, the sunrise ceremonies there, and the strict beauty of the Western Shoshone washes, hills, and mountains:

> *Participating with awareness*
> *In the Great Cycle of*
> *Nurturing and Being Nurtured*

After this repetitive introductory statement, phrases follow that represent the understanding I have gleaned from Rolling Thunder and numerous other Elders. Sample statements pertaining to my discussion above are:

- *Participating with awareness in the Great Cycle of Nurturing and Being Nurtured,* I am aware of the power of words and the realities they create. I dedicate myself to mindfulness in the use of all of my words.

- *Participating with awareness in the Great Cycle of Nurturing and Being Nurtured,* I notice the suffering brought about when we impose our views on others.

- *Participating with awareness in the Great Cycle of Nurturing and Being Nurtured,* I notice how my personal patterns may shield me from the surrender and vulnerability necessary for receiving the gifts of nurturing through my medicine.

- *Participating with awareness in the Great Cycle of Nurturing and Being Nurtured,* I see how attachment and addiction to views and perceptions create limitations and imbalance.

- *Participating with awareness in the Great Cycle of Nurturing and Being Nurtured,* I see that I am only in this life and body because of all my ancestors.

RT was at the early beginnings of the road that led me to remember what it might mean for me today to live within an indigenous understanding of the world. Without the inspiration and challenges he presented, and without the limitations he embodied, I might not have arrived where I am today. My deep gratitude goes to him, Spotted Fawn, the people at Meta Tantay who welcomed me, and the land on which we celebrated the sunrise ceremony.

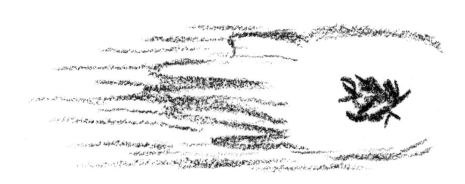

Every physical object in nature has a spiritual side. Therefore, these objects can be spiritual helpers to the medicine man.

ROLLING THUNDER

Rolling Thunder Was a Social Networker

Sidian Morning Star Jones

SIDIAN MORNING STAR JONES, Rolling Thunder's grandson and one of the caretakers of his spiritual legacy, is a graphic designer, inventor, and founder of My Mythos (mymythos.org), a website that allows people to compare their personal myths. He is also the founder of Open Source Religion (www.opensourcereligion.com), a platform to help people define and refine their beliefs. Coauthor of *The Voice of Rolling Thunder* with Stanley Krippner, he lives in Boise, Idaho.

Long before the pervasive connectivity of the Internet of today, it is said that shamans all over the world maintained connection with one another. Even from far corners of the world, folklore holds that they communicated by nontraditional means. In a loose parallel with quantum physics, one might call this "spooky action at a distance," a phrase famously coined by Albert Einstein, who was both suspicious of, and wrong about, the subject.

Amaro Laria, a psychiatrist from Boston, once traveled to a jungle village in Ecuador. When he said he was from the United States, the village shaman asked, "Do you know Stanley Krippner?" In fact, Amaro did. Sometime later, Amaro was in central Java. Again, a shaman asked, "If you are from America, perhaps you know Stanley Krippner." Amaro could hardly believe it when the same question was asked a third time by a shaman in a Brazilian rain forest. Dr. Krippner is quite connected, but was there something more to the event?

Stanley had a similar experience himself in 1980 when he was in South Africa visiting the legendary Zulu shaman Credo Mutwa. Stanley noticed that the shaman was wearing a large turquoise necklace and asked who had given it to him. Credo Mutwa replied, "It was from a friend of Rolling Thunder, who is a Native American medicine man." When Stanley revealed that he was a longtime friend of RT, Credo Mutwa was surprised, saying, "I have heard all about you from Rolling Thunder's friend. Please stay and help us celebrate the coming decade."

During the festive celebration, there was drumming, chanting, singing, and the traditional "throwing of the bones." Credo Mutwa interpreted the arrangement of the bones to indicate that Nelson Mandela would become president of South Africa. Few people believed that this would be possible, but the prophecy was fulfilled.

Leslie Gray, who is both a licensed clinical psychologist and a Native American shaman, told me that my grandfather was a talented organizer, especially when it came to warning people about the coming ecological crisis. He would say, "Wake up. The Earth is in peril. We are not taking care of her." Unfortunately, this prophecy is being confirmed today as well.

Dr. Gray also told me that my grandfather felt that there was a role that technology could play. Indeed, Meta Tantay was run by wind and solar power. The community used solar power to heat water for their warm showers, wash the dishes, and do the laundry. RT helped install this technology himself. Many of the young people who came to Meta Tantay went on to have great careers in the computer industry, social networking, environmental technology, and alternative energy production.

It is a bit of a paradox to contemplate how a rustic Native American medicine man could have had such an impact on twenty-first-century technology. But he did.

Smoke and Mirrors

Steve Speer

STEVE SPEER has been involved with the mystical aspects of technology and media for more than three decades. As a pioneering computer animator, he colonized a vacant cyberspace with his 3D creations. As a writer he has written for, among others, *Wired Magazine* and *Feral House's Apocalypse Culture 2*. He is the author of *The Celestial Clockwork* and was born and continues to live in New York City. He can be reached at reepss@aol.com. In this chapter, Speer draws upon his knowledge of mythology and magic to augment Krippner's description of how myths led to science and how magical practices led to technology. He associates the Aztec use of obsidian ("the smoking mirror") with Sidian Jones's name (and expertise with computers). He sees echoes of Mesoamerican symbolism in Rolling Thunder's heroic journey, replete with initiatory snakes and trickster coyotes. He also proposes that cyber shamanism might alleviate Rolling Thunder's fear that Western science and technology have run amok to the detriment of nature, including human beings.

The serpent is a labyrinth, coiled and convoluted, and those who walk the serpent's path are sometimes shamans. All of them know that only the bravest, the wisest, and the luckiest can complete the shaman's journey. The stakes are high, given that the soul itself hangs in the balance.

A sense of doubt will beset those who begin the journey. Once inside the maze, all sense of direction disappears. The goal itself seems occluded, yet amid the growing confusion, the explorer is inexplicably pulled toward greater mysteries. Every step leads to another threshold beyond which secrets are hinted to lie. Paths are tested as the labyrinth unfolds, exciting the senses with the promise of wonderful rewards ahead. Mistakes are made. And only when all progress seems thwarted, when the initiate is thrust into the hopelessness of innumerable dead ends, are valiant efforts rewarded.

Is this not similar to the confusion experienced when learning how to operate a new piece of tech gadgetry? Twists and turns and impasses are met when one is confronted with an arcane device, and there is exhilaration, triumph, and relief when the veil is parted. And finally you have gotten the browser Safari to run on your iPhone 6! The dark mirror of tablets and phones do indeed reflect the labyrinth, with its threat of losing one's way—first amid manuals and tutorials, then amid the deeper, perhaps more occult revelations of the technology. It may seem that the stakes that come from toying with a smartphone or an iPad are not so high, but it is said that if you play, you pay, and there are always other forces at work.

The purveyors of such gadgetry are intent on finding new ways to lure their customers in and to keep the cycle of buying and discarding in effect. With the purchase of each new device consumers are forced to "shed the skin" of their old gadget and the hard-earned lessons on how to use it, and begin again the process of acquisition and disposal. A continual initiation is set in place, an initiation into the useless mysteries of ever-newer devices whose gimmicks and features become increasingly redundant and time-consuming.

Only the priesthood of the new fad gadgets reap their profits. For the consumer, the cycle leads nowhere; it is an ouroboros where no ground is gained and consumers begin again from where they started, only now with empty wallets and increasingly deadened souls. And as the users go further into the labyrinth of technology, as they submerge themselves deeper into the dark pool of the screen, for good or ill, nature is left behind.

THE CROSSROADS OF NATURE AND TECHNOLOGY

The meeting with a new technology is a crossroads where a choice is offered. If the contract is accepted, the password will be granted. Thresholds are reached and portals are opened, but it has often been observed that doors open from both sides. The mirror has two faces. The crossroads reached at present could be said to be one of nature and technology. For some, this seems a trivial matter, one of no consequence. But for those who care to notice, the massive shift in the zeitgeist resulting from this juncture is astounding. A new type of *magik*, wild and reckless, is happening where digital technology and the occult meet. But just who is the guardian of this crossroads and which trickster has pointed the way?

Rolling Thunder was known to call up rainstorms to erase any sign of the rituals he had performed, knowing that the smallest traces left behind still had magical power that would best not be used by malevolent forces. Protection against harm when performing any magical act has historically been of utmost importance. Before a magician or a shaman would attempt contact with entities from beyond ordinary nature they would traditionally go through a period of purification and prayer in preparation for such contact. Precautions were taken so that whatever entity might appear would not gain undue influence over the practitioner's will, or, even worse, displace her soul.

QUETZALCOATL AND HIS BROTHER TEZCATLIPOCA

In the Native American pantheon some deities are well-known, while others are clouded in mystery, shadow, and smoke. For many, Quetzalcoatl is among those best-known, but what about the others? There are always lurkers at the threshold and perhaps it is the Lord of the Obsidian Mirror who now is at the door.

In his introduction to this book, Stanley Krippner proposed that magic became technology and myth became science. "However," he continues, "technology without a touch of magic becomes mechanistic and science without a mythic subtext becomes materialistic. Mechanism and materialism have brought Earth and its inhabitants to a critical point in history." Perhaps this critical point, this crossroads, is one where the vast curvaceous vistas of the natural world have been supplanted by horizons limited to the dark angled surface of smartphones. In ages past these devices, shorn of the World Wide Web and its digitized connectivity, would have been recognized as useful for scrying. Had an American Indian of past centuries been presented with such a device they would have immediately recognized the slab of dark glass as one of Tezcatlipoca's magical obsidian mirrors.

Quetzalcoatl was recognized by Native Americans as a culture bearer, the bringer of the dawn, the prompter of wisdom and learning, and a friend of humankind. He is the one whom Rolling Thunder envisioned as a golden snake capable of initiating humans into a broader awareness of their plight. And as Rolling Thunder was initiated into the mysteries of Quetzalcoatl, the bright plumed serpent, so are billions, while under a technological trance, now being unwittingly initiated into a contract with his brother, Tezcatlipoca, so long denied proper recognition.

In Aztec mythology the enigmatic Tezcatlipoca is the trickster par excellence. His name means "Smoking Mirror," but he was also known, among almost 130 titles, as "The Enemy of Both Sides," "The Lord of the Near and Far," and "Him through Whom We Live." The god of sin, misery, and sorcery, he is also the patron of Aztec kings and politicians.

He represents change through conflict and is the god of war. Even though he was the adversary of his brother, the far more renowned Quetzalcoatl, they joined forces to create the world. While doing so, Tezcatlipoca used his foot as bait to lure the monstrous crocodile Cipactli from the sea in hopes of using its enormous body as land for the newly formed planet. Cipactli took the bait, devouring Tezcatlipoca's foot. The foot was replaced, oddly, with an obsidian mirror. That mirror is in some representations swapped for a snake. As the lord of the smoking mirror Tezcatlipoca uses the dark glass surface of obsidian to see and be seen as if the mirror served as some magical surveillance technology, one with which he could spy upon his subjects. Along with jaguars, snakes and coyotes are two of Tezcatlipoca's most prominent totem animals.

It is intriguing to wonder what Rolling Thunder himself thought of Tezcatlipoca. While the brightly plumed Quetzalcoatl is an easy sell, having been suitably homogenized for safe consumption by the New Age, Tezcatlipoca is something different. Darker and more enigmatic, he poses no easy answers. While Quetzalcoatl offers a safe flirtation with shamanism, most novices seeking a feel-good experience would most likely not want to know of the more dangerous elements that lurk about. However, enantiodromia, the tendency of things to move from one extreme to the other, is rarely thwarted, especially in mythology.

Although Rolling Thunder was initiated by a snake, he maintained a long rapport with coyotes, and this alone would place him in the vicinity of Tezcatlipoca's realm. And as Rolling Thunder chronographically stood astride the age that was, and the "New Age" of technology, perhaps he was more of a transitional figure than has previously been imagined.

THE DARK MIRROR AND THE THREAT
OF TECHNOLOGY

The similarities between the surface of the English magus John Dee's obsidian scrying mirror, Tezcatlipoca's mirror, and the surface of any smartphone or tablet are apparent. It is believed that John Dee's scrying mirror, which remains on prominent display at the British Museum, was gifted to him by Sir Francis Drake. Drake procured the mirror on one of his voyages, possibly directly from the Aztecs, or perhaps from a cargo of booty taken from a Spanish armada. Whatever the means by which he gained possession, the mirror was in fact a sacred Aztec ritual item used to invoke the presence of Tezcatlipoca, the Lord of the Smoking Mirror. And who cannot say that it was Tezcatlipoca who counseled John Dee from the black glass to set in motion the beginnings of the British Empire "whose dark satanic mills" Blake's inklings recognized as the first signs of the global transformation in which we find ourselves complicit?

As Rolling Thunder performed rituals for the purpose of requesting that the local coyotes keep the local rabbit population down, it needs to be asked, What is the purpose of the ritual of the obsidian mirror? What purpose is there in having most of the world's population enslaved by the need to peer, again and again, into the dark glass? And if it is the plumed serpent's downcast brother who leads us into that mirror, whose smoking fumes pass like clouds before our eyes, just what is his agenda?

Now the dark mirror has achieved a ubiquity perhaps beyond any other, where in nearly every pocket around the globe rests this talismanic scrying tool. Perhaps the use that we imagine this tool is present to perform is not indeed the reason why that tool was brought here. It is a testament to the haunting power of obsidian, and its long hold over the minds of men and women, that Rolling Thunder's own grandson and coauthor of this book, Sidian Morning Star, has taken a name that echoes that of the dark volcanic glass.

Carl Jung, in his brilliant and prescient essay "Wotan," postulated that a psychic force could sometimes, at moments of crisis, rise and seize the reins of human development. He spoke of the potential for "a totality on a very primitive level, a psychological condition in which man's will was almost identical with the god's and entirely at his mercy," where the Ergriffener (one who is seized) is under total control of the Ergreifer (one who seizes).

I ask, as you read Jung's statement, to substitute the name of the agenda-driven Germanic entity with an equally agenda-driven Mesoamerican one: "As an *autonomous* psychic factor, Wotan produces effects in the collective life of a people and thereby reveals his own nature. For Wotan has a peculiar biology of his own, quite different from the nature of man."

It is precisely the nature of man at stake here, as the supernatural force of Tezcatlipoca sweeps across the planet, supplanting the flora and fauna, the four elements, the lightning and the thunder for a shard of dark mirror from which floods a hypnotic overload of media. The information thus transmitted, truly no more than flashing zeroes and ones, is widely agreed to be disproportionately trivial, useless, and largely obscene. Is it no less apparent that this immersion wholeheartedly into the haze of digital effluvium, evidenced by the oblivious masses wandering streets with their attentions undividedly affixed on tiny little screens, pecking at breadcrumb trails as they enthusiastically declaim the most banal of personal vanities, is somehow affecting their very souls? Will there not be, with the psychic strain of such wide-scale mediumship, a steep price to pay? And what will be the toll?

In his interview with Jean Millay, Rolling Thunder addressed this threat in the piece "Life Should Be Beautiful for Everyone." He said, "All this pollution comes from the minds of modern people. Their brains are cluttered up with trash or worse—aggression, greed, and fear. The human brain is so big, and has so much capacity, but if it's cluttered up with trash and limited in narrow ways of thinking, it can't have room to create the good things."

As contemporary culture wanders deeper into the labyrinth of manufactured meaning, consumerism, and self-surveillance, the question remains: Who benefits? And to what end? It has often been said that people are becoming enslaved to the technology they have invented. Another of Tezcatlipoca's monikers was "He to Whom We Are Slaves."

For initiation to impart true knowledge of the human condition, it must be not just cyclical but helical. Like the coiled serpent, it proceeds upward and with every turn progress is made. To accept initiation is to know that other initiations will follow, that the search will continue. But this occurs on another level, where meaning has deepened and spiritual truths have been learned.

TEZCATLIPOCA'S STRENGTHENING PRESENCE

With the shamanism of practitioners like Rolling Thunder seemingly fading from the world, perhaps there is a new current, to use the jargon of the pundits, a cyber shamanism. And with the dominance of this shamanism, the old ways, the ways of nature, will fade too. What will fill the void? The optimism of the '80s and '90s was bolstered by the hope that digital innovations would lead to a Cyberdelic Age, a utopian age of magical technology. These hopes were best exemplified in the influential magazine *Mondo 2000,* but as the digital revolution progressed and the smell of money permeated the water, the sharks circled.

The venture capitalists and money changers who commercialized the temple were willing to sell both their and their customers' souls for a few dollars more. With that, the cyberdelic dreams of creative freedom and greater awareness withered. Crass commercialism won out.

John Crowley, in his Aegypt series of four novels, hypothesized an event where all that was known before was suddenly gone, supplanted by a new paradigm of both physics and beliefs. Those who had gone through that change and those who came after both had, at best, scant memories of the age that had preceded them. What had gone before was thought of as legend, with all of legend's accompanying magic and wonder. Are we in such a period now where a new myth will topple the old? One where the golden light of Quetzalcoatl will be exchanged for the smoke and mirrors of Tezcatlipoca? And could this type of dramatic shift resonate with what futurists imagine as "the Singularity"? Will the singularity of Tezcatlipoca be one of complete control governed by encroaching technologies? The transhumanist movement, which ties its goals to technological advances, would have us move from human to something beyond. In truth this might end up being not human at all. If the basis of humanity is the soul, then I can imagine no better way to strip the soul from the body, to cast out the self, than by narrowing humanity's perceptions down to a few inches of dark glass.

According to Stanley Krippner, a ritual performance can either open new horizons for the future or close them down. At this juncture, where it seems that no one can find the means to fully gauge the situation, is the embrace of the technological ritual of the smoking mirror, "Him to Whom We Are Slaves." Will this lead us to a brighter future or to a dismal end in dehumanized enslavement?

Has authentic experience been lost amid the swirl of information? So much of what the digital revolution has foisted is useless for those seeking awareness, for discovering truths. The aesthetic of the shaman seems to have been washed away in the tidal wave of bits and bytes that have deluged the infosphere and threatens the mythscape. The immediate experience of nature has been exchanged, at the crossroads, for the safer mediated experience, where life is experienced as a reflection, an eidolon, on a screen. As cybernetician Gotthard Günther has stated, "reflection is repetition."

Overall, almost 48.9 million metric tons of used electrical and electronic products were produced in 2012, an average of 15.4 pounds for each of the world's 7 billion people. If the legacy of Tezcatlipoca is smoldering mountains of electronic debris as far as the eye can see, slowly leaching into the Earth their poisons of lead, mercury, and arsenic, then what is to be gained? Is there, in these dark mirrors, a hint of the numinous? Or is this the greatest trick of the greatest trickster, who has lain so long patiently in wait for the proper moment when technological advances finally reach the point where his plan might come to fruition?

But perhaps the greatest catastrophe that comes about with the wanton and thoughtless use of the technology of the smoking mirror will be the loss of soul. As memory and experience are increasingly mediated through the interface of dark glass, who cannot resist the notion that the way people are connecting with each other has all changed, changed utterly? Do people meet anymore in communal gatherings, or is the new mediation of the screen now the preferred mode of social engagement?

Hints of Tezcatlipoca's strengthening presence can be glimpsed in the media. A cult hit on the BBC is *Black Mirror*. Charlie Brooker, the show's creator, describes it thus: "If technology is a drug—and it does feel like a drug—then what, precisely, are the side-effects? This area—between delight and discomfort—is where 'Black Mirror,' my new drama series, is set. The 'black mirror' of the title is the one you'll find on every wall, on every desk, in the palm of every hand: the cold, shiny screen of a TV, a computer monitor, a smart phone."

Corinthians I (13:12), in the King James Version of the Bible, says this: "For now we see through a glass, darkly; but then face to face: now I know in part; but then shall I know even as also I am known." What could this strange language of St. Paul's mean? The American gnostic Philip K. Dick was so struck by it that he paraphrased it for his novel *A Scanner Darkly,* which dealt with the despair of technological surveillance. Can we so easily dismiss the archetypal presence of Tezcatlipoca, whose creeping malevolence is everywhere around us? Is it possible that in all the jabber about the trickster, in all the theorizing of what the trickster might signify, the trickster has gone about his business and now the trick is done?

As a young man, Rolling Thunder was called by Quetzalcoatl to enter a shining golden portal and become a healer of men. Today many people are answering a call that has led them headlong into the depths of Tezcatlipoca's dark mirror. They do this without proper training and engage with preternatural forces unwittingly. The cosmic battle that has so long been waged for humanity's soul is regarded as of little importance.

Recently, I found myself in discussion with a hip young woman about technology and its potential dangers. I mentioned how for the first time in history, technology has become available for the complete control of the financial system. This control, I continued, could be accomplished along the lines of the biblical mark of the beast. I elaborated on how, in the book of Revelation, only those who took the mark and complied with the worldwide governance of the great beast would be able to buy or sell in that New World Order. She laughed, and her reply was chilling. "If it makes it easier for me to shop, what do I care about my soul?"

In closing, again I will cite Jung's "Wotan": "But what do all the beauties of the past from totally different levels of culture mean to the man of today, when confronted with a living and unfathomable tribal god such as he has never experienced before? It has always been terrible to fall into the hands of a living god."

As Cormac McCarthy wrote in the classic book *Suttree,* it is often the ruder forms that survive.

Bibliography

Allen, Paula Gunn. *Off the Reservation*. Boston: Beacon Press, 1998.

Arthritis Foundation. "Predict Your Joint Pain Level Based on the Local Weather." www.arthritis.org/living-with-arthritis/tools-resources/weather. Accessed March 4, 2015.

Barnosky, Anthony D., et al. "Approaching a State Shift in Earth's Biosphere." *Nature* 486 (June 7, 2012): 52–58.

Boyd, Doug. *Rolling Thunder: A Personal Exploration into the Secret Healing Powers of An American Indian Medicine Man*. New York: Random House, 1974.

Bruyere, Rosalyn. *Wheels of Light: Chakras, Auras, and the Healing Energy of the Body*. New York: Touchstone Publishing, 1994.

Campbell, Joseph. *Transformations of Myth through Time*. New York: Harper Perennial, 1999.

Cardeña, Etzel, Steven Lynn, and Stanley Krippner. *Varieties of Anomalous Experience: Examining the Scientific Evidence*. 2nd ed. Washington, D.C.: American Psychological Association, 2013.

Chief Seattle. *California Indian Education*. www.californiaindianeducation .org/famous_indian_chiefs/chief_seattle. Accessed April 20, 2016.

Corntassel, Jeff, and Richard Witmer. *Forced Federalism: Contemporary Challenges to Indigenous Nationhood*. Norman, Okla.: University of Oklahoma Press, 2008.

Feinstein, David, and Stanley Krippner. *Personal Mythology: Using Ritual, Dreams, and Imagination to Discover Your Inner Story*. 3rd ed. Santa Rosa, Calif.: Energy Psychology Press/Elite Books, 2008.

Friedman, Harris, and Glenn Hartelius, eds. *The Wiley-Blackwell Handbook of Transpersonal Psychology.* Oxford, UK: Wiley-Blackwell, 2013.

Glover, Jerry, and Harris Friedman. *Transcultural Competence: Navigating Cultural Differences in the Global Community.* Washington, D.C.: American Psychological Association, 2015.

Gong, Tommy. *Bruce Lee: The Evolution of a Martial Artist.* 2nd ed. Valencia, Calif.: Black Belt Communications, 2014.

Gray, Leslie. "The Looks-Within Place." In *Moonrise: The Power of Women Leading from the Heart,* edited by Nina Simons with Anneke Campbell. Rochester, Vt.: Park Street Press, 2010.

Günther, Gotthard. *Idea and Outline of a Non-Aristotelian Logic, Vol. 1: The Idea and Its Philosophical Postulates.* Hamburg, Germany: Meiner, 1957.

Harner, Michael. *Cave and Cosmos: Shamanic Encounters with Another Reality.* Berkeley, Calif.: North Atlantic Books, 2011.

Hunt, Valerie, et al. *A Study of Structural Integration from Neuromuscular, Energy Field, and Emotional Approaches.* Boulder, Colo.: Rolf Institute of Structural Integration, 1977.

Intergovernmental Panel on Climate Change. *Climate Change 2014 Synthesis Report.* (November 2014). www.ipcc.ch/pdf/assessment-report/ar5/syr /SYR_AR5_FINAL_full_wcover.pdf. Accessed August 19, 2014.

Jones, Sidian Morning Star, and Stanley Krippner. *The Voice of Rolling Thunder: A Medicine Man's Wisdom for Walking the Red Road.* Rochester, Vt.: Inner Traditions, 2012.

Jung, Carl. "Wotan, Civilization in Transition." In *The Collected Works of C. G. Jung, Vol. 10,* Princeton, N.J.: Princeton University Press, 1978.

Kremer, Jürgen Werner, and R. Jackson-Paton. *Ethnoautobiography: Stories and Practices for Unlearning Whiteness Decolonization Uncovering Ethnicities.* Sebastopol, Calif.: ReVision Publishing, 2014.

Kremer, Jürgen Werner, et al. "Coming to Presence." In *Proceedings of the 18th International Conference on the Study of Shamanism and Alternate Modes of Healing* (2001): 233–241.

Krippner, Stanley. "Psychology of Shamanism." In M. N. Walter and E. J. Neumann Fridman, eds., *Shamanism—An Encyclopedia of World Beliefs, Practices, and Culture.* Santa Barbara, Calif.: ABC-CLIO, 2004.

Krippner, Stanley, and Alberto Villoldo. *The Realms of Healing.* Millbrae, Calif.: Celestial Arts, 1976.

Krippner, Stanley, and Harris Friedman, eds. *Mysterious Minds: The Neurobiology of Psychics, Mediums, and Other Extraordinary People.* Santa Barbara, Calif.: Praeger, 2010.

Laughlin, Charles D. *Communing with the Gods: Consciousness, Culture, and the Dreaming Brain.* Brisbane, Australia: Daily Grail, 2011.

Lévi-Strauss, Claude. *The Savage Mind.* Chicago: University of Chicago Press, 1966.

Luscombe, Belinda. "Half-Chippewa Novelist Louise Erdrich on Her Crime Thriller, Geronimo's Name and the Good Ideas of Richard Nixon." *TIME* (January 24, 2015): 60.

———. "Native American Poet and Author Sherman Alexie on Rain Dances, Alcoholism and Chief Wahoo." *TIME* (October 29, 2012): 76.

Lyon, William S. *Spirit Talkers: North American Indian Medicine Powers.* Kansas City, Miss.: Prayer Efficacy Publishing, 2012.

Lyons, Charles. "Suicides Spread through a Brazilian Tribe." *New York Times Sunday Review* (January 4, 2015): SR6.

McCarthy, Cormac. *Suttree.* New York: Vintage Books, 1986.

Mijares, Sharon, et al. *The Root of All Evil.* Exeter, UK: Imprint Academic, 2007.

Nez, N. "The Myth of the Rain Dance." *Skeptical Beliefs* (Spring 2013): 9–11.

Olivier, Guilhem. *Mockeries and Metamorphoses of an Aztec God: Tezcatlipoca, "Lord of the Smoking Mirror."* Boulder, Colo.: University Press of Colorado, 2008.

Pachauri, Rajendra K. *Report of the 40th Session of the IPCC* (October 27–31, 2014). www.ipcc.ch/meetings/session40/final_report_p40.pdf. Accessed April 27, 2016.

Pope, Carmen, ed. *Rolling Thunder Speaks: A Message for Turtle Island.* Santa Fe, N.Mex.: Clear Light. 1999.

Rees, Sir Martin. In *Quantum Enigma: Physics Encounters Consciousness.* B. Rosenblum and F. Kuttner, eds. New York: Oxford University Press, 2006.

Saint Germain, Carolyna. *Stewards for the Earth.* Bloomington, Ind.: Balboa Press, 2014.

Sala, Luc. *Ritual: The Magical Perspective.* Hilversum, Netherlands: Mindlift Publishers, 2014.

Sanders, Robert. "Scientists Uncover Evidence of Impending Tipping Point for Earth." University of California—*Berkeley News Center.* http://newscenter.berkeley.edu/2012/06/06/scientists-uncover-evidence-of-impending-tipping-point-for-earth. Accessed June 6, 2012.

Schwartz, Stephan A. Quoted in "The Mist Wolf" in *The Voice of Rolling Thunder.* Sidian Jones and Stanley Krippner. Rochester, Vt.: Bear & Co., 2012.

"Social Scientists Build Case for 'Survival of the Kindest.'" *Science Daily.* www.sciencedaily.com/releases/2009/12/091208155309.htm. Accessed December 9, 2009.

"State of the Climate." *NOAA National Climatic Data Center.* www.ncdc.noaa.gov/sotc/. Accessed June 10, 2012.

Swan, Jim. *Sacred Places: How the Living Earth Seeks our Friendship.* Santa Fe, N. Mex.: Bear & Company, 1990.

Swinney, Graywolf. "Beyond the Vision Quest: Bringing It Back or Did I Really Ask for This?" *Dream Network Journal* 11 (2) (1992): 17–19.

Thompson, William Irwin. *The Time Falling Bodies Take to Light: Mythology, Sexuality, and the Origins of Culture.* New York: St. Martin's Press, 1981.

Wikihow. "How to Predict the Weather without a Forecast." www.wikihow.com/Predict-the-Weather-Without-a-Forecast. Accessed March 1, 2015.

Wilkins, David. *American Indian Politics and the American Political Systems.* New York: Rowan and Littlefield, 2010.

Willerslev, Rane. *On the Run in Siberia.* Minneapolis, Minn.: University of Minnesota Press, 2012.

———. *Soul Hunters.* Berkeley, Calif.: University of California Press, 2007.

Yates, Frances. *The Occult Philosophy in the Elizabethan Age.* New York: Routledge & Kegan Paul, 1983.

Yong, Ed. "Life Found Deep inside Earth's Oceanic Crust." *Scientific American.* www.scientificamerican.com/article/life-found-deep-inside-earths-oceanic-crust/. Accessed November 25, 2014.

Index

BOOKS OF RELATED INTEREST

The Voice of Rolling Thunder
A Medicine Man's Wisdom for Walking the Red Road
by Sidian Morning Star Jones and Stanley Krippner, Ph.D.

Original Instructions
Indigenous Teachings for a Sustainable Future
Edited by Melissa K. Nelson

Speaking with Nature
Awakening to the Deep Wisdom of the Earth
by Llyn Roberts and Sandra Ingerman

Walking on the Wind
Cherokee Teachings for Harmony and Balance
by Michael Tlanusta Garrett

Medicine of the Cherokee
The Way of Right Relationship
by J. T. Garrett and Michael Tlanusta Garrett

Sacred Plant Medicine
The Wisdom in Native American Herbalism
by Stephen Harrod Buhner

Becoming Nature
Learning the Language of Wild Animals and Plants
by Tamarack Song

Iroquois Supernatural
Talking Animals and Medicine People
by Michael Bastine and Mason Winfield

INNER TRADITIONS • BEAR & COMPANY
P.O. Box 388 • Rochester, VT 05767
1-800-246-8648
www.InnerTraditions.com

Or contact your local bookseller